Germanic Warrior AD 236–568

Simon MacDowall • Illustrated by Angus McBride

First published in Great Britain in 1996 by Osprey Publishing,
Midland House, West Way, Botley, Oxford OX2 0PH, UK
44-02 23rd St, Suite 219, Long Island City, NY 11101, USA
Email: info@ospreypublishing.com

Transferred to digital print on demand 2010

First published 1996
11th impression 2009

Printed and bound by Cadmus Communications, USA

A CIP catalogue record for this book is available from the British Library

ISBN: 978 1 85532 586 9

Editorial by Iain MacGregor
Design by The Black Spot
Filmset in Great Britain by KDI, Newton le Willows

Acknowledgements
Special thanks to Peter Sautter for his excellent line drawings.

Artist's Note
Readers may care to note that the original paintings from which the colour plates in this book were prepared are available for
private sale. All reproduction copyright whatsoever is retained by the Publisher. Enquiries should be addressed to:

Scorpio Gallery
PO Box 475
Hailsham
East Sussex
BN27 2SL

The Publishers regret that they can enter into no correspondence upon this matter.

The Woodland Trust
Osprey Publishing is supporting the Woodland Trust, the UK's leading woodland conservation charity, by funding the
dedication of trees.

www.ospreypublishing.com

GERMANIC WARRIOR AD 236 – 568

INTRODUCTION

The 3rd to the 6th centuries saw the collapse of the classical Mediterranean civilisation and the emergence of new states in western Europe based on the Germanic warrior society. It is not the purpose of this book to trace the fascinating evolution from classical to feudal society, but rather to look at the man who was perhaps the most important player in this process: the Germanic warrior. This book will examine the warrior society of the Germans, looking at how the men lived and fought. The emphasis is on the individual warrior rather than the great events of the time. It is focused particularly on the men who made up the retinues of the Germanic warlords who carved kingdoms out of the carcass of the West Roman Empire.

There were a great many individual German tribes living beyond the Roman Empire at the start of this period, and they certainly did not think of themselves as one people. The same language root was probably all that many of these diverse people had in common. Even then it is doubtful that a Frank living along the Rhine could have made himself understood by a Goth on the banks of the Dniester.

The Migrations changed much of this. External and internal pressures destroyed tribal unity and replaced it with multi-national bands of warriors following powerful warlords. The Visigoths, for example, were made up of two breakaway clans of Goths reinforced by Romans, Huns, Alans, Sarmatians and Taifals; and the Merovingians were a mix of Franks, Burgundians, Romans, and Alamanni. Likewise, Roman armies could be made up almost entirely of Germans. Even at much lower levels, the retinues of the individual Germanic warlords were not built up on the old clan or tribal system. Young men seeking their

German captives from a Roman monument. Roman propaganda tended to portray the Germans as naked savages. (Peter Sautter)

fortune would come from far and wide to join the warband of a successful leader. Warfare of this period was not between national groupings, but between various bands of warriors of similar backgrounds following different leaders. These competing bands fought to secure land and wealth for themselves and to increase their power and prestige; when a leader lost his luck and reputation, many of his followers would drift away to join another who offered greater prospects.

In looking at how the Germanic warrior of the Migrations lived and fought, it is possible to take a general view. Differences in tactics, equipment and lifestyle were more dependent on time and place than on national characteristics. For example, a Goth who remained on the eastern

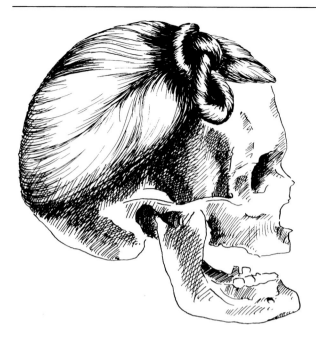

A German warrior's skull from northern Germany, showing the 'Swabian knot' hairstyle – see Plate A. (Peter Sautter)

Steppes after the arrival of the Huns was more likely to fight mounted than his cousin who fled to the sanctuary of the Roman Empire. It is not possible in the scope of this book to examine in detail the fine differences of equipment and tactics of all the Germans during the Migrations, but it is possible to give a generalised overview, and to look at what motivated the average German warrior fighting in the ranks of a multi-national retinue, and, to see how his fighting methods evolved over the centuries.

CHRONOLOGY

(Major battles in bold)

236-68 Franks, Alamanni and Goths overrun Rhine and Danube frontiers.

251 Roman army defeated by Goths at **Forum Terebronii**.

268-80 Roman frontiers restored.

313 Edict of Milan brings recognition for Christianity throughout the Roman Empire.

355-60 Frankish and Alamannic expansion west of the Rhine is checked by the Romans under Julian.

357 Alamanni defeated at the **Battle of Strasbourg**.

368-69 Raids of Saxons, Picts and Scots in Britain.

370-75 Alans and Goths conquered by the Huns.

376 Crossing of the Danube by Gothic refugees.

378 East Roman army destroyed by Goths at **Adrianople**. Emperor Valens killed.

382 Goths given land to settle along the Danube frontier.

394 Theodosius' East Roman army, including a large number of Goths, defeats the Western army of Arbogast at **Frigid River**.

401-04 Inconclusive campaign between the Goths and Romans as the Goths look for land to settle.

405-06 Vast German migration led by Radagaisus defeated by the Romans.

406-10 Vandals, Suevi, Alans and Burgundians cross the frozen Rhine and overrun Gaul and Spain.

407 Roman troops leave Britain.

410 Visigoths under Alaric sack Rome.

413 Burgundians settle near Worms.

414 Visigoth campaign against the Vandals, Alans and Suevi in Spain.

419 Visigoths establish independent kingdom in southern Gaul and Spain.

429 Vandals and Alans cross from Spain into Africa.

431 Failed joint east-west Roman campaign against Vandals in Africa.

433-50 Campaigns of Aetius against Visigoths, Franks and Burgundians in Gaul. Hunnic auxiliaries in the Roman army defeat the Burgundians near **Worms**, killing King Gunther (celebrated in the *Niebelungenlied*).

443 Surviving Burgundians re-settled in Savoy.

449 Traditional date for the start of Anglo-Saxon settlement in Britain.

451 Hun invasion of the West checked by an army of Visigoths, Franks, Romans and Burgundians under Aetius at **Campus Mauriacus**.

455 Vandal sack of Rome.

476 Barbarian mercenaries in the Roman army

depose the Emperor Romulus Augustulus. Odoacer becomes ruler of Italy.

481 Accession of Clovis.

486 Clovis' Franks defeat the Gallo-Romans under Syagrius and consolidate their hold on northern France.

488-93 Ostrogoths invade and conquer Italy.

496 Clovis' Franks defeat the Alamanni.

498 Franks become Catholic Christians.

507 Franks under Clovis defeat the Visigoths at **Vouillé** in southern France.

533-34 Vandal north African kingdom destroyed by the East Romans under Belisarius.

534 Burgundians conquered by the Franks.

534-54 Gothic War. Italy is devastated by wars between the East Romans, Goths and Franks.

565 Lombards and Avars destroy the Gepid Kingdom.

568 Lombards invade Italy.

THE WARRIOR SOCIETY

The characteristics of Germanic warfare
In the 1st century AD the Roman historian P. Cornelius Tacitus described the society of the pre-migration Germans. What he described was a warrior society in which war was one of the central elements and the only manly occupation:

'A German is not so easily prevailed on to plough the land and wait patiently for harvest as to challenge a foe and earn wounds for his reward. He thinks it spiritless to accumulate slowly by the sweat of his brow what can be got quickly by the loss of a little blood.

'When not engaged in warfare they spend a certain amount of time hunting, but much more in idleness, thinking of nothing else but sleeping and eating. For the boldest and most warlike men have no regular employment, the care of house, home and fields being left to the women, old men and weaklings of the family.'

The kind of warfare that fuelled and maintained this society was different from that which a Roman might have understood. There were no equivalents to the life and death struggles between Rome and Carthage, where the aim became the total destruction of an enemy society. Early Germanic warfare, like that of most warrior societies, was almost a ritual part of life. Struggles between families or clans were to accumulate wealth and prestige, or exact revenge for previous successes by an opponent, rather than the total defeat and destruction of the enemy. Weapons and tactics were relatively simple, and although their battles would cause casualties, they were unlikely to be massive.

Contact with the advancing Romans had many effects on Germanic society: warfare certainly became more deadly; weapons and equipment

Marcomannic chieftains surrendering to Marcus Aurelius at the end of the 2nd century. These are probably fairly realistic representations of Germanic warriors, although they have been stripped of their weapons and armour. (Musei Capitolini, Rome)

This very wide 4th-century warrior's belt from Dorchester is typical of the style worn by German and Roman soldiers of the time. It is 10cm wide with bronze stiffeners and attachments. The rings at the top left possibly supported a shoulder belt while the bottom ring could have been for a knife or purse. In the 4th century both the Germans and the Romans wore their swords on the left-hand side, possibly from a baldric over the right shoulder. Another possibility however, is that the sword was slung from a thinner secondary belt attached to the main belt from the ring on the right-hand side and hanging down on the left hip. (Ashmolean Museum, Oxford)

improved; and those Germans living close to the Rhine found themselves having to fight for survival. As a result small tribes and clans began to coalesce into loose confederacies such as the Franks and Alamanni and were thus able to draw on a much larger pool of manpower. Many Germans saw service in Roman armies, and although relatively few of them eventually returned to Germania at the end of their service, some did. Such men would have accumulated wealth beyond the wildest dreams of those who had stayed behind, thus elevating them to positions of prominence.

They also brought back with them the Roman ideas on command and control, and it is no surprise that the great early German war leaders such as Marobodus and Arminius had seen service in Roman armies.

Although Roman ideas of command and control could never be completely imposed on a heroic warrior society, contact with Rome saw the erosion of a tribal system and its gradual replacement by men of wealth and power who gathered followers from across tribal lines and maintained them through success in war. These great men and their followers evolved into the kings and nobles of early medieval society.

LEADERSHIP AND HIERARCHY

Far from being the democratic society of warrior farmers of popular myth, the Germans were already developing a hierarchy based on military prowess in Tacitus' day:

'There are grades of rank even in these retinues determined at the discretion of the chief whom they follow; and there is great rivalry, both among the followers to obtain the highest place in their leader's estimation and among the chiefs for the honour of having the biggest and most valiant retinue. Both prestige and power depend on being continually attended by a large train of picked young warriors which is a distinction in peace and a protection in war.'

Over the period of the Migrations the power

and strength of the chiefs and their retinues grew. A leader departing his homeland left behind the communal life of the clan. He took with him his *comitatus*: adventurous and capable followers who would depend on the leader for their livelihood. Property in a migrating people could no longer be land held in common; rather it became portable wealth held by the leader and distributed to his loyal followers.

The land settlements made by the Romans were often dealings with the great leaders who were treated as commanders of allied armies. Once settled, these men inherited parts of the Imperial bureaucracy and began to surround themselves with regal trappings; then their power became more absolute and arbitrary. Gregory of Tours describes a scene when Clovis, king of the Franks, assembled his warriors to share out booty and asked that he be allowed a ewer, over and above his normal share:

'They listened to what he said and the more rational among them answered: "Everything in front of us is yours, noble King, for our very persons are yours to command. Do exactly as you wish, for there is none among us who has the power to say nay." As they spoke, one of their number, a feckless fellow, greedy and prompt to anger, raised his battle-axe and struck the ewer. "You shall have none of this booty," he shouted, "except for your fair share." ... At the end of the year he [Clovis] ordered the entire army to assemble on the parade ground, so that he could examine the state of their equipment. The King went around inspecting them all and finally came to the man who had struck the ewer. "No other man has equipment in such a bad state as yours," he said. "Your javelin is in a shocking condition, and so are your sword and your axe!" He seized the man's axe and threw it to the ground. As the soldier bent forward to pick up his weapon, King Clovis raised his own battle-axe in the air and split his skull with it. Clovis ordered the others to dismiss. They were filled

Feasting played an important role in the life of the Germanic warrior. This spit was buried with a Frank in the 6th century near Krefeld. (Peter Sautter)

with mighty dread at what he had done. Clovis waged many wars and won many victories.'

This passage is illustrative not only of the growing arbitrary power of the kings and war leaders but also of how this power rested on strength, violence, and success in war. A leader showing weakness or allowing a challenge to go unanswered would soon be usurped by a stronger man, and removed from his position of power.

It is also interesting to see that such an obviously Roman concept as a parade ground inspection had been adopted by the Franks as early as the end of the 5th century. If we contrast

A fine jewelled fibula worn by the head of a Retinue, and probably of Alammanic origin. (Musée Archéologique Strasbourg)

This reconstruction of a Frankish warrior is based on typical grave contents found in the middle Rhine area.
(Museum Burg Linn, Krefeld)

Gregory's passage with one from Tacitus several centuries earlier, we can see that the military basis for Germanic society had changed a great deal over the intervening centuries:

'The power even of the kings is not absolute or arbitrary. The commanders rely on example rather than on the authority of their rank. Capital punishment, imprisonment, even flogging, are allowed to none but the priests, and are not inflicted merely as punishments or on the commanders' orders, but as it were in obedience to the god whom the Germans believe to be present on the field of battle.'

The retinues

Tacitus implies that all German men in his day carried arms and as such could be considered warriors. In the early days of the Migrations when whole peoples were on the move across Europe, it is quite possible that this was still sometimes the case. Many of the peoples who settled and established themselves within the Roman Empire were

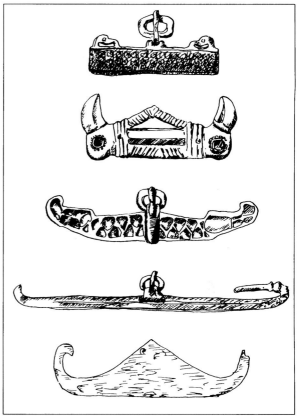

One of the warrior's important possessions would have been a piece of steel to use with a flint to start a fire. These fire steels would have been attached by the buckle to the warrior's belt. ((Peter Sautter, after Christlein)

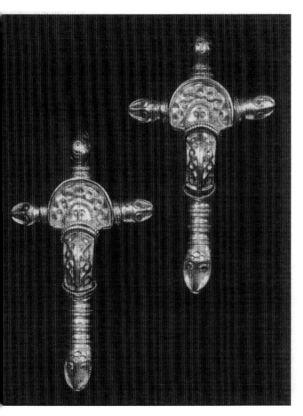

th century Frankish brooches made of gilded silver, a style widespread in the Germanic world. (Museum Burg Linn, Krefeld)

bands of fighting men of mixed ancestry, who carved out a territory and then set themselves up as a warrior aristocracy. They provided the fighting men while the Romans continued to run the non-military activities.

Apart from the epic struggles with the Romans, such as the Gothic war in Italy, warfare in the Germanic kingdoms was characterised by raids and dynastic squabbles. This low intensity conflict did not require every able-bodied man to rally to his people's defence: rather, it was more suited to small bands of semi-professional retainers, bound by oaths of loyalty to their chief, fighting to increase his power and prestige.

The warriors who filled the ranks of these retinues were often recruited from across tribal lines of wealth and class. Tacitus says: 'Many noble youths, if the land of their birth is stagnating in a long period of peace and inactivity,

A replica of the seal ring of the early Frankish king Childeric, which was found together with a large hoard of fine weapons and jewellery. The original, along with many other items, was stolen last century.
(Ashmolean Museum, Oxford)

deliberately seek out other tribes which have some war in hand.' The heroic poetry of the age is filled with examples of this, such as Siegfried arriving at the Burgundian court in the *Niebelungenlied*, or *Beowulf* and his followers being welcomed by the Danish king's attendant who remarks: 'I have never seen a larger or bolder company of newcomers; and I am sure it is out of daring and the spirit of adventure, not because of exile or banishment, that you have come.'

A young man joining the retinue of a war leader would be looking for a chance to establish a reputation and accumulate wealth. The chieftain would reward his services by providing his upkeep and presenting him with gifts. In Beowulf, the Danish King Hrothgar is called the 'giver of rings', and after defeating Grendel, *Beowulf* and his followers are presented with gifts of a staggering value:

'Hrothgar gave Beowulf an embroidered banner of gold, a helmet and a corselet, in reward for his victory. Multitudes saw the jewel-studded sword of honour presented to the hero. Beowulf drank a ceremonial cup in the banqueting hall, for the gifts were so costly that in accepting them he need feel no shame before the fighting men.... Hrothgar ordered eight horses with golden bridles to be led into the

courtyard... the king of the Danes now delivered th horses and weapons into the keeping of Beowulf an told him to use them well. Thus the renowned princ guardian of the soldiers' treasury, repaid Beowulf f his combat with Grendel in horses and gold, with generosity which every honest man must approve.

The King also presented over the banqueting tab some valuable old heirlooms to each of those who ha crossed the sea with Beowulf, and ordered compensation to be paid for the man whom Grendel ha wickedly killed.'

The giving of costly gifts would enhance the reputation of the giver as well as the receiver. As th reputation increased, more men would seek hi out and his war band would grow, along with h chance of success in war. Hrothgar, for exampl had 'such success in arms and so great a fame that 'his kinsmen were eager to serve under hi and in this way the number of his young retaine increased until he had a formidable army'. Thi as Tacitus noted, would produce a never endin cycle of petty violence:

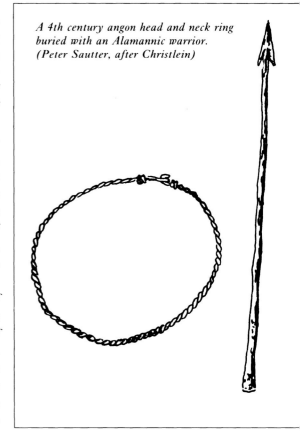

A 4th century angon head and neck ring buried with an Alamannic warrior.
(Peter Sautter, after Christlein)

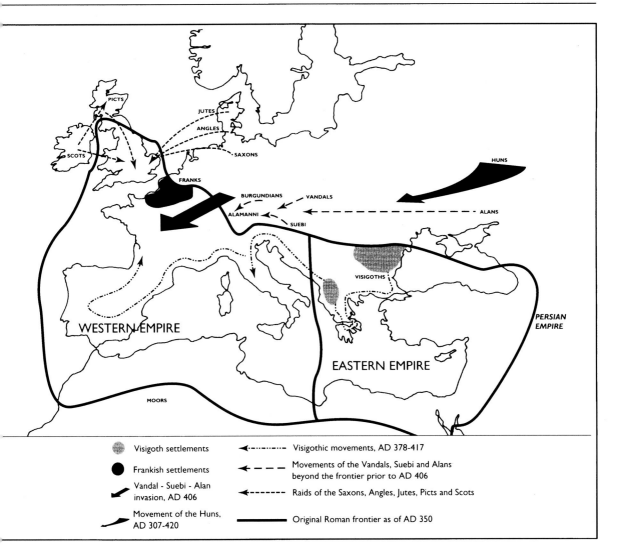

◯ Visigoth settlements	◀·—·—·— Visigothic movements, AD 378-417
● Frankish settlements	◀— — — Movements of the Vandals, Suebi and Alans beyond the frontier prior to AD 406
◀ Vandal - Suebi - Alan invasion, AD 406	◀------- Raids of the Saxons, Angles, Jutes, Picts and Scots
◀ Movement of the Huns, AD 307-420	▬▬▬ Original Roman frontier as of AD 350

A large body of retainers cannot be kept together except by means of violence and war. They are always making demands on the generosity of their chief, asking for a coveted war-horse or a spear stained with the blood of a defeated enemy. Their meals, for which plentiful if homely fare is provided, count in lieu of pay. The wherewithal for this open-handedness comes from war and plunder.'

The code of loyalty

The warrior was bound to his lord through a code of loyalty. Tacitus says that 'the chiefs fight for victory, the followers for their chief'. The chief, as the strongest and most able warrior, led by example. The followers had to 'defend and protect' the chief, never deserting him and fighting to the death if necessary since 'to any

This map shows the Visigothic invasion and some of the main barbarian movements up to the early 5th-century.

fighting man death is better than a life of dishonour' (*Beowulf*). An example of this was noted by Ammianus Marcellinus after the defeat of the Alamanni at the Battle of Strasbourg in AD 357. The defeated King Chnodomar and his *comitatus* attempted to evade pursuit but were cut off and surrounded by the Romans. Chnodomar, accepting the inevitable, 'came out of the wood alone and gave himself up. His attendants to the number of 200, together with three very close friends, also surrendered, considering it a disgrace to survive their king or not to die for him if the occasion required it'.

Attitudes regarding the duty of a retainer to his

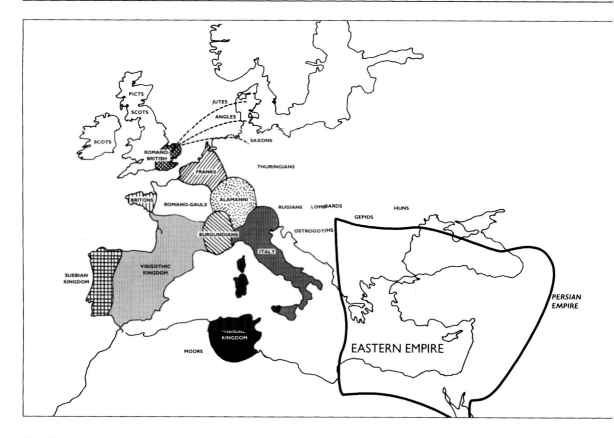

The Germanic successor kingdoms after the fall of the western Roman Empire in AD 476.

chief changed little over the centuries. The same concepts first described by Tacitus can be found many centuries later. Gregory of Tours writing in the 6th century tells the story of a Frankish chief in northern France called Ragnachar, 'who was so sunk in debauchery that he could not even keep his hands off the women of his own family'. Clovis, seeing an opportunity here for advancement, bribed Ragnachar's *leudes* (personal retainers) with gold arm bands and sword belts to turn against their chief.

This succeeded and Clovis was able to defeat Ragnachar in battle. Clovis' reaction when Ragnachar and his brother Ricchar are bound and brought before him are illustrative of Germanic attitudes towards the responsibilities and duties of a chief and his followers:

'Why have you disgraced our Frankish people by allowing yourself to be bound?" asked Clovis. "It would have been better for you had you died in battle." He raised his axe and split Ragnachar's

skull. Then he turned to Ricchar and said: "If y had stood by your brother, he would not have be bound in this way." He killed Ricchar with a seco blow of his axe. When these two were dead, th who had betrayed them discovered that the go which they had received from Clovis was counterfe When they complained to Clovis, he is said to ha answered: "This is the sort of gold which a man c expect when he deliberately lures his lord to death He added that they were lucky to have escaped wi their lives instead of paying for the betrayal of th rulers by being tortured to death.'

Another example of the Germanic warrior co of loyalty can be found in 8th century Angl Saxon England when Prince Cyneheard took h revenge on King Cynewulf of Wessex who h deposed Cyneheard's brother. Having learned th the king was visiting his mistress with only a fe of his retinue in attendance, Cyneheard plann an ambush. The king was killed, but his me were roused by his lady's screams and rushed avenge their dead lord. Cyneheard offered to b them off but 'none of them would accept, b they went on fighting continuously until they

This typical Late Roman sword could easily have found its way into the hands of a Germanic warrior. (Roemisch-Germanisches Zentral Museum, Mainz)

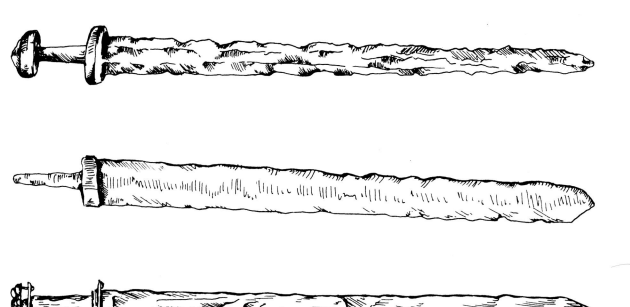

These Frankish and Alamannic swords are typical of the styles produced by German smiths in the Migration period. (Peter Sautter)

ay slain'. The following day, the remainder of the ing's retinue arrived to find Cyneheard in a for- ified position:

'[Cyneheard] *offered them their choice of money and land if they would grant him the kingdom, and told them that kinsmen of theirs were with him who would not desert him; and they replied that no kinsman was dearer than their lord, and they never would follow his slayer; and then they* [the king's men] *offered to let their kinsmen depart unharmed. And they* [the kinsmen] *replied that the same had been offered to their comrades who had been with the king; and then they themselves did not care for this "any more than your comrades who were slain with the king". And they* [the king's men] *went on

fighting around the gates until they forced their way in and slew the prince and the men who were with him.'* (Anglo Saxon chronicle)

This example, although from a later period, shows that the bonds between the ideal warrior and his lord could be even stronger than blood ties, even leading to inevitable death.

There is a danger that we develop a romanticised view of the Germanic warrior from these stories, which portray the ideal values a warrior would strive for. If Roman armies depended on drill and discipline for cohesion (and the clan groupings of the early Germans had the natural solidarity of kinship), the codes of loyalty were the bonds that held together the men in the *comitatus* of a Migration period war-leader. As in all armies, reality did not always live up to the ideal, and the Germans duly had their share of shirkers, coward's, thieves and traitors. Beowulf, for example, is in the end deserted by 'cowardly runaways who had not the courage to lift a spear when their leader was in trouble'.

A sampling of some of the laws of the Visigoths show us that the Germanic warrior suffered from the same fears and temptations as any other man in war:

'If a thiufadus [commander of a "thousand"] is bribed by a man from his unit [thiufa] to permit him to return home, he would render to the count of the city in whose district he was stationed what he had accepted ninefold.'

'If a centenarius [officer of a "hundred"] abandoning his unit [centena], deserts to his home, he will be executed.'

'As many times as an attack of the enemy is launched against our kingdom some so scatter themselves at the quickest opportunity, relying on change of location, malicious hate and even the pretence of their incapacity, that in that struggle of fighting th one does not expend fraternal aid to the other.'

TRAINING

We know very little of how warriors were traine or even if any formal training was carried ou Most likely, young boys would imitate the fathers and be taught the warrior's skills by h family. A life based on subsistence agriculture an hunting would have kept most young men phy ically fit, and it is quite likely that their ski were honed by various sports and games. Sidoni Apollinaris says of the Franks, for example, th 'it is their sport to send axes hurling through th vast void and know beforehand where the blo will fall, to whirl their shields, to outstrip wit leaps and bounds the spears they have hurled, an

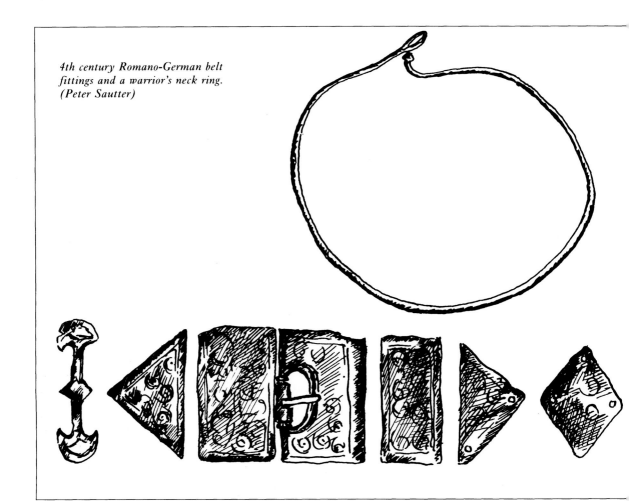

4th century Romano-German belt fittings and a warrior's neck ring. (Peter Sautter)

This highly decorated gold and garnet sword knob is typical of an almost universal Germanic aristocratic style. The interlocking rings may have symbolised the bond between the warrior and his lord. (Museum Burg Linn, Krefeld)

This iron disc decorated with silver and brass was probably used to connect straps forming part of a horse's harness. (Deutcher Kunstverlag, from the Praehistorische Staatssammlung, Munich)

each the enemy first. Even in boyhood's years the love of fighting is full-grown'. Tacitus also briefly mentions a display in which 'naked youths, trained to the sport, dance about among swords and spears levelled at them. Practice begets skill and grace; but they are not professionals and do not receive payment'. Games such as these, together with hunting, would have taught the young warrior the basic individual weapons handling skills he would need to survive.

There is no indication, however, that any kind of unit or formation training was carried out by any of the Germans. A young warrior on his first campaign would probably accompany his relatives and stand in a rear rank where all he had to do was follow the actions of others. Gradually, if he survived, he would acquire greater experience until he would be in a position to pass on his skills to other younger men.

EQUIPMENT AND APPEARANCE

Manufacture of weapons

'The Germans wear no breast plates or helmets. Even their shields are not reinforced with iron or leather, but are merely painted boards. Spears of a sort are limited to the front rank. The rest have clubs, burnt at the ends or with short metal points...' (Germanicus)

'Even iron is not plentiful; this can be inferred from the sort of weapons they have. Only a few of them use swords or large lances.' (Tacitus)

These statements represent the Roman image of the early Germans: poorly equipped and lacking the skills to produce high quality metal goods. This idea of the half naked savage with primitive weapons was further enhanced by the propaganda of Roman triumphal arches and monuments,

This jewel decorated the sword scabbard of a well-to-do 6th-century Frank. (Museum Burg Linn, Krefeld)

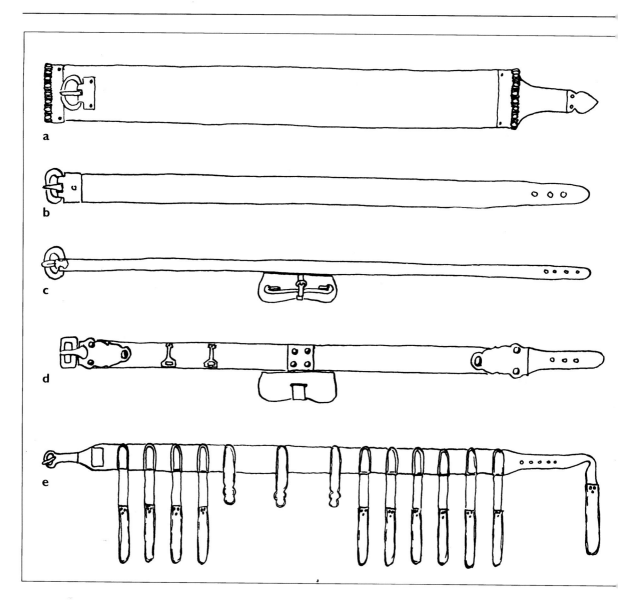

Belt styles evolved during the Migrations: a) 4th century; b) 5th century; c) 6th century; d) 6th century; e) 7th century. (Peter Sautter)

which inevitably showed the Germans, stripped of their weapons and armour, either kneeling in supplication or being ridden down by victorious Roman cavalry.

Compared to the heavily armoured 1st-century legions of professional soldiers, the weapons of the German tribes may indeed have seemed poor. But most would not have been full-time warriors, and consequently would have had little need to equip themselves with much more than a spear and a shield. The wars with Rome and the growth of

the *comitati* saw German armies containing an ever increasing number of well-equipped full-time warriors, and although plunder would greatly increase their arsenals, they were not totally dependent on Rome for high quality weapons.

Despite Tacitus' inference, there were extensive, accessible iron deposits throughout Germania, and archaeologists have found evidence of sizeable workshops in production from the 1st century. One workshop, in what is now Poland, shows evidence of over 150 smelting furnaces indicating fairly sophisticated centralised production. Furthermore, the skills of Germanic smiths and other craftsmen were as good as, or better than those found inside the Roman Empire

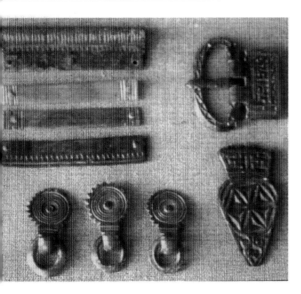

...th-century bronze belt stiffeners, buckles and attachment ...ngs from Germany, very similar to those found at ...orchester. (Museum Burg Linn, Krefeld)

...he magnificent gold and garnet decorated ...quipment and pattern welded blades are clear ...vidence of their abilities and certainly surpass the ...ass produced weapons of the Late Roman *...bricae* (arms factories). Such a comparison is not ...ompletely fair, since the *fabricae* were having to ...quip hundreds of thousands of Roman soldiers ...hile the *comitatus* of a powerful Germanic chief ...ight only number in the hundreds. But as the ...ermanic armies evolved into warrior aristoc-...acies, it would not have been unusual for the ...quipment of a Germanic warrior to equal or ...urpass that of an average Roman soldier.

Once inside the Empire, much or all of the ...arrior's equipment could come from Roman ...ources. The Gothic refugees who crossed the ...anube in AD 376 probably had only basic ...quipment, but after their great victory at ...drianople they would have had access not only ...o battlefield booty but also to weapons stored in ...he region. Later, when bands were employed *en ...asse* as *federates* in the Roman armies, they ...ould have had access to the Imperial *fabricae.*

Alaric's Visigoths who sacked Rome in AD 410 ...lternated between roles as Roman soldiers and ...nemies. Alaric was appointed master of soldiers ...*magister militum*) in the Balkans in AD 397, and ...oasted of his control of the Illyrian *fabricae*; the

soldiers that he led must have been very well equipped indeed.

General appearance

The Germanic warrior during the Migrations often carried his wealth on his person. The warrior's status was measured by his success in war, and this could be visibly demonstrated by the quality of his equipment, which might be booty from a defeated enemy or the gift of a grateful chief. There was no such thing as a uniform in this disruptive period, even among the Romans: each man equipped himself as best he could. The better, and therefore most successful, warriors might be fully equipped with brightly coloured and decorated clothes, horse, armour, helmet, sword, spear, axe and shield; poorer men, or those yet to establish a military reputation, would have no armour and be equipped only with a spear and shield. In some armies, notably the Alamanni and Goths, poorer men often served as archers.

The basic clothing of nearly all Germans throughout this period and beyond was a tunic and trousers, over which a cloak was worn in inclement weather. Agathius' description of the Franks as 'clad in close-fitting garments with a belt around the waist' is confirmed by a number of surviving garments which have been found in peat bogs in northern Germany and Denmark. These include long-sleeved, knee-length tunics with slits at the wrists to allow the hand through

Typical 6th-century belt fittings. Rich men often had the metalwork on their belts richly decorated in niello and silver or gold. (Museum Burg Linn, Krefeld)

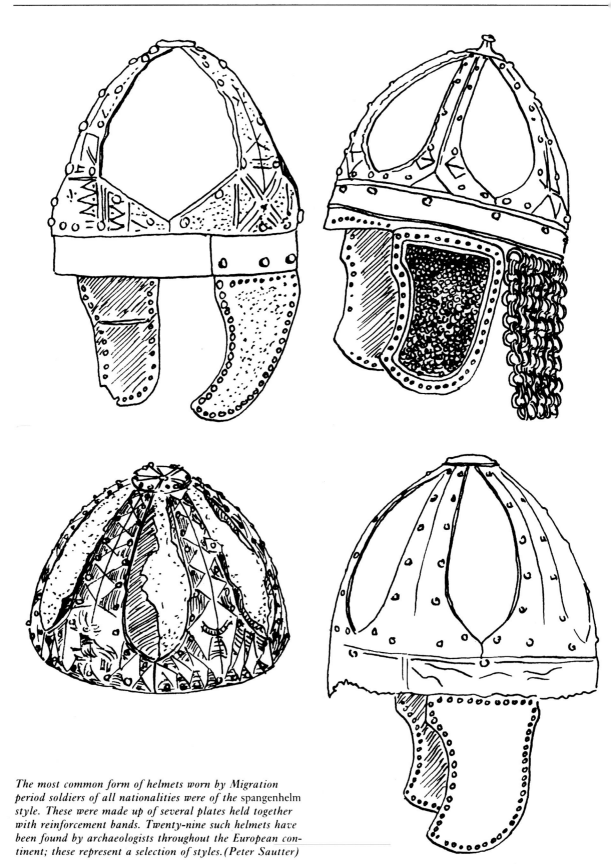

The most common form of helmets worn by Migration period soldiers of all nationalities were of the spangenhelm *style. These were made up of several plates held together with reinforcement bands. Twenty-nine such helmets have been found by archaeologists throughout the European continent; these represent a selection of styles. (Peter Sautter)*

nd tight hose with enclosed feet. Sometimes
ooser short-sleeved tunics were worn over a long-
leeved shirt, and the lower legs were usually
ound with wrap-around puttee-like bindings.

Clothing was usually wool, but linen was also
orn, as was a wool-linen mix. Belts were a uni-
ersal item of military dress and served to indicate
he wearer's status as a warrior. In the 4th century
hese belts could be extremely wide and were
itted with buckles and loops to attach equipment
uch as a sword, a purse, and a firesteel. There
vere, of course, variations in fashion that changed
vith time and place. The Visigoths, for example,
vere quick to adopt Roman-style dress, while
nany eastern Germans, such as the Gepids and
)strogoths, would have worn the looser fitting
arments of the Steppe peoples.

Sidonius Apollinaris, writing in the mid-5th
entury, gives several detailed descriptions of the
'ranks, which give us a good idea of the
Germanic warrior seen through Roman eyes:

*'Their eyes are faint and pale, with a glimmer of
reyish blue. Their faces are shaven all round, and
nstead of beards they have thin moustache's which
hey run through with a comb. Close-fitting garments
onfine the long limbs of the men; they are drawn up
o high so as to expose the knees, and a broad belt
upports their narrow waist.'*

*'The most gracious sight of the procession was the
rince himself, marching on foot amidst his runners
nd footmen, clad in gleaming scarlet, ruddy gold and
ure white silk, while his fair hair, glowing cheeks*

*This Frankish gravestone is one of the very few represen-
tations of a Germanic warrior not made by the Romans. A
large Sax features prominently at his belt, and he is
apparently combing his hair.
(Peter Sautter, from the Niederdollendorf stone)*

*Many helmets had additional neck protection, often of
ink-mail. This 4th-century helmet plate was found rusted
ogether with some mail, probably indicating a neck guard.
St Irminen, Trier)*

*and white skin matched the colours of his bright dress.
The chiefs and companions who escorted him presented an aspect terrifying even in peacetime. Their
feet from toe to ankle were laced in hairy shoes;
knees, shins and calves were uncovered: above this
was a tight-fitting many coloured garment, drawn up
high and hardly descending to their bare thighs, the
sleeves only covering the upper part of the arm. They
wore green mantles with crimson borders. Their swords
suspended from the shoulders by baldrics pressed
against sides girded with studded deerskins. This
equipment adorned and armed them at the same time.
Barbed lances and throwing axes filled their right
hands; and their left sides were protected by shields,
the gleam of which, golden on the central bosses and*

6th-century Germanic spearheads. These could be quite long and heavy. The winged spearhead on the left, for example, is 35cm long. The long narrow heads would probably have been fairly good at piercing armour. (Deutcher Kunstverlag, from the Praehistorische Staatssammlung, Munich)

silvery white around the rims, betrayed at once the ruler's wealth and ruling passion.'

The second passage is particularly interesting on a number of counts. There is, for example, a hint of uniformity in the description of the green and crimson mantles, and also in the silver and gold decorated shields. This might be expected in the comitatus of a wealthy prince, who would have presented his followers with some clothing in order to display his wealth and power. Gifts of clothing, for example, are noted by Procopius being presented to Roman allies. The bare legs described by Sidonius are not attested anywhere else: all other evidence points to tight trousers or hose being worn by the western Germans. However, bare legs with wool socks bound up to the knee in a cross-garter pattern are commonly shown in Roman mosaics from the period, especially those showing agricultural workers. This style might possibly have been adopted by the Franks and other Germans in hot weather. The silver- or iron-bound shields are also not widely attested, metal shield fittings found in Germani graves are limited to the central boss, hand gri and some decorative panels. The edges were mor commonly bound with leather.

Armour
Modern ideas of the Germanic warrior' equipment have been influenced by Roma writers and grave goods found by archaeologists We have already seen the false impression Roma writers have given us of the Germans' materia wealth, and we must bear in mind that in additio to being propagandists, most Roman writers ha never seen a German except, perhaps, as a captiv or as a mercenary. Archaeology reveals to us wha a given warrior was buried with; this does no necessarily mean that his grave goods represente his entire military panoply.

Armour and swords are notoriously time-con suming, and therefore expensive to produce. Onl the fabulously wealthy could afford to be burie with them, but this does not mean that others di not have them. The poem *Beowulf*, for example, i filled with references to armour:

'Each tough hand-linked coat of mail sparkled and the shimmering ringlets of iron clinked in thei corselets.'

'Bloodstained corselets, iron helmets with golde

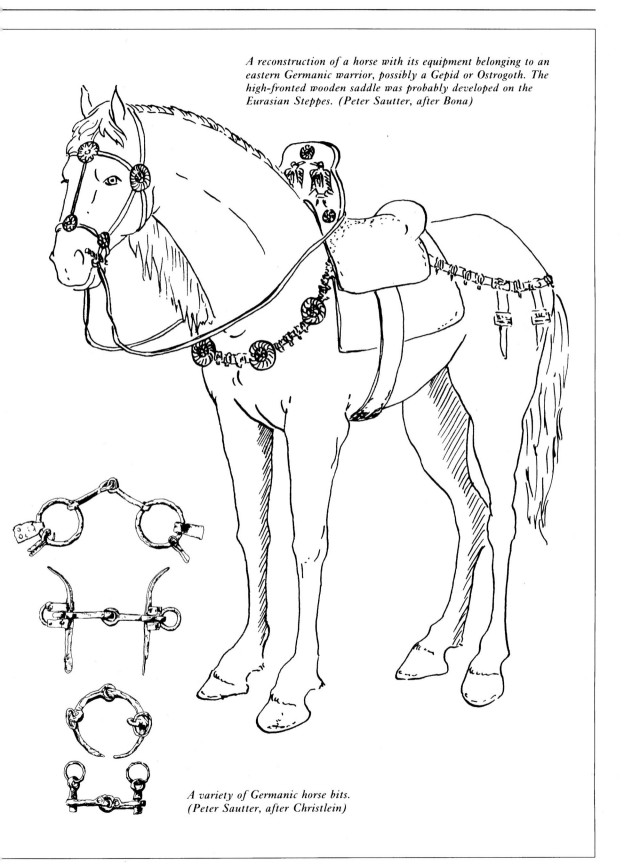

A reconstruction of a horse with its equipment belonging to an eastern Germanic warrior, possibly a Gepid or Ostrogoth. The high-fronted wooden saddle was probably developed on the Eurasian Steppes. (Peter Sautter, after Bona)

A variety of Germanic horse bits.
(Peter Sautter, after Christlein)

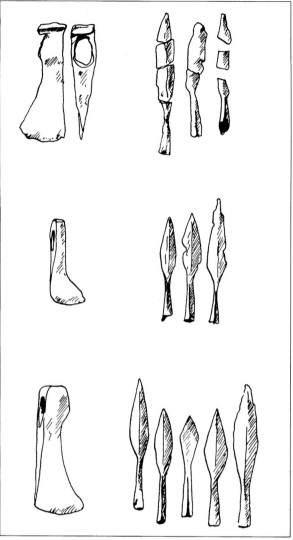

Three sets of similar weapons; buried with, what would seem to be judging by their contents, fairly poorly equipped 4th-century Alamannic warriors. (Peter Sautter, after Christlein)

Germans were ill equipped. His frequen[t] descriptions of battles between Romans an[d] Germans are usually presented as a contest [of] equals when it comes to equipment. Usin[g] classical literary tradition, he presents th[e] Germans as wild and headstrong, contrasting th[em] to the steady, cautious Romans, but when it com[es] to equipment, the two are portrayed as equal. [He] makes reference to Germans being weighed dow[n] by their arms, and during the Battle of Adrianop[le] he describes 'helmets and breast-plates' being sp[lit] asunder on both sides.

One reason why a warrior might not be burie[d] with some of his equipment is that some of th[e] more expensive items would have been presente[d] to him by his leader, and technically were not h[is] to dispose of. It was customary for a warrio[r]

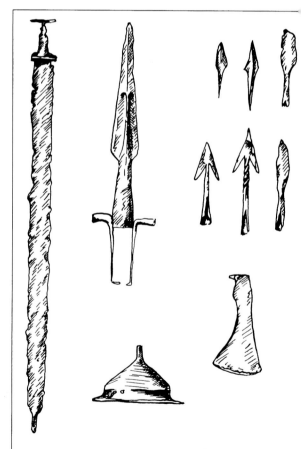

A full range of typical 5th-6th century Alamannic weapon[s] including arrow and javelin heads, a sword, francisca, spiked shield boss and a large heavy boar-hunting spear. (Peter Sautter, after Christlein)

boar crests and numbers of dead chieftains were plainly to be seen on the pyre, for many notable men had fallen in battle.

'At their heads they set their bright shields, and on the bench above each chieftain, the towering helmet, corselet of link-mail, and huge spear were plain to see. It was their practice to be ready to fight at any moment, whether at home or abroad, whenever occasion arose and their commander needed them.'

Ammianus Marcellinus, a 4th-century Roman officer, does not convey the impression that the eaving the service of a leader to return equipment that he had received. The family of a warrior who had died might also be expected to return such items to the leader, who would in all likelihood present them back to a surviving son.

Those men who owned expensive items like body armour would normally keep them in the family, like Beowulf, who says:

'*If I am killed in combat, send to Hygelac* [Beowulf's uncle] *the coat of mail which I am wearing. For it is the best corselet in the world, the work of Weland Smith, and an heirloom that once belonged to my grandfather Hrethel.*'

It is highly likely, therefore, that a warrior serving in a chieftain's *comitatus* would have worn some form of body armour in addition to a helmet and shield. This might have been stripped from a defeated enemy on the battlefield, issued from a Roman *fabrica*, given as a gift by a chief, or produced to order by a German smith.

Ring mail was the most common type of armour, but other forms were also possible. Towards the end of this period, iron lamellae, which had been introduced from the east, became increasingly popular, and remnants of impressive lamellar panoplies have been found in Frankish and Alamannic graves. Some form of leather armour may also have been worn. We have already seen the mention by Sidonius Apollinaris of 'studded deerskins', although these may refer to the very wide leather utility belts worn in this period. There are also indications that the 7th-century Angle King, buried at Sutton-Hoo, had a leather breastplate in addition to a mail shirt.

THE WARRIOR ON CAMPAIGN

Campaign limitations

The Germanic warrior was a skilled individual fighter, brave, loyal and confident in his abilities. His idea of war, however, was a quick raid, perhaps culminating in a single glorious battle, and then a return to celebrate or mourn in the

These two Frankish leather shoulder bags would have been useful for carring rations and small items of personal equipment. (Museum Burg Linn, Krefeld)

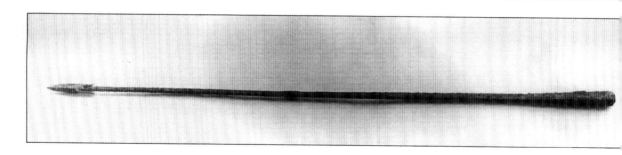

An iron angon head from France. The angon, similar to the Roman pilum, was possibly a prestige weapon. (British Museum, London)

great hall. He was notoriously reluctant to spend a protracted time in the field if he could avoid it, and as a result, when matched against Roman opponents, initial success frequently gave way to eventual defeat.

The strengths of the German in battle and his weaknesses on campaign were well known to the Romans, and exploited by them. The *Strategikon*, a 6th-century military manual, gives a Roman commander the following advice on 'dealing with the light-haired peoples such as the Franks, Lombards and others like them':

'They are disobedient to their leaders. They are not interested in anything that is at all complicated and pay little attention to external security and their own advantage. They are hurt by heat, cold, rain, lack of provisions, especially of wine, and postponement of battle. They are easily ambushed along the flanks and to the rear of their battle line, for they do not concern themselves at all with scouts and the other security measures. Above all, therefore, in waging war against them one must avoid engaging in pitched battles, especially in the early stages. Instead, make use of well planned ambushes, sneak attacks and stratagems. Delay things and ruin their opportunities. Pretend to come to agreements with them. Aim at reducing their boldness and zeal by shortage of provisions or the discomforts of heat or cold.'

Although war was an integral part of Germanic life, major campaigns were infrequent and brief. Cattle rustling, petty raids and competition between rival warbands characterised their ideal of warfare. A sustained campaign requires full-time soldiers and organised logistics. This the Germans did not have, and their society was not geared to

produce them. When the circumstances were right the Germans could and did wage protracted campaigns, but these were usually forced upon them either by outside attack or by a desire to find land to settle.

As long as things were going well, a German chieftain had a reasonable chance of maintaining an army in the field. But his followers were looking for booty and glory, and this could only be won through victory. As soon as it appeared that these would not be forthcoming, momentum would be lost and the campaign would quickly collapse. Without a bureaucracy and cash economy to back them up, Germanic armies could not hope to develop more than the most basic logistics. Consequently, offensive armies had to be small and mobile, and able to live off the land if need be. A warlord with a *comitatus* of a few hundred excellent fighting men, well equipped and mounted, could hope to accomplish more than one burdened with extra mouths to feed that did not significantly increase his combat capability.

The Germans were also notoriously bad at siege warfare. They could not maintain a large army in one place long enough to starve out a determined town and the small aristocratic warbands were not suited to the drudgery of a protracted siege. Towns did fall to them, but usually only if the defenders gave up quickly. The description of the Alamannic attempt to capture Sens in 356 is perhaps typical when 'after a month the barbarians withdrew dispirited, complaining that it had been futile and foolish to think of besieging a town'. (Ammianus Marcellinus)

Life on campaign

To illustrate the life of a typical warrior on campaign at the height of the Migrations, let us follow the exploits of a hypothetical Goth who crosses into the Roman empire as an 18-year-old in AD 376. He is perhaps one of the Tervingi, a Gothic confederacy who in the 370s were living in what is now Ukraine and Moldova.

He had probably had his first experience of war a few years earlier, defending his homeland against the onslaught of the Huns. On his first campaign he would have had only the most basic equipment: a spear and shield given to him by his family and perhaps a knife. Unless his family was rich, he probably went on foot and 'took up his position in a good spot near the banks of the Dniester', while more experienced warriors went twenty miles ahead to watch for the approach of the enemy'. (Ammianus Marcellinus)

The result of the battle would have been a terrifying introduction to combat. The Huns bypassed the advance guard, forded the river by moonlight and launched a surprise attack on the unsuspecting Goths. Ammianus tells us that the Goths were driven off with the first onset and took refuge in some rugged mountain country'. It is easy to imagine the fear that the surprise attack would have inspired, followed by a hasty retreat

with no supplies, harried along the way by fast moving bands of Hunnic horse archers. Once in the tenuous security of the rougher terrain, our man, together with other lesser warriors, was probably put to work building a long line of fortifications which the Gothic leader, Athanaric, hoped would help hold back the Huns. But having suffered defeat, Athanaric began to lose his prestige and authority. After his experiences in his first battle, and being young and unmarried, our man was probably easily convinced to follow Alavivus and Fritigern who broke away from Athanaric and moved west to seek refuge inside the Roman Empire.

We know little of the trek west, but it must have been under arduous conditions. Supplies would have been scarce after the war with the Huns, and Ammianus tells us that the Tervingi were 'weakened by the necessities of life'. Foraging would have been difficult for people moving with entire families, together with all their belongings, and they would have been very vulnerable to any attack by the Huns. On reaching the Danube, they would have had to wait for

This selection of combs and ear-cleaning spoons were found in Gepid graves. Personal hygiene tools were commonly buried with men and women, giving lie to the Roman idea of the Germans as unkempt savages. (Peter Sautter)

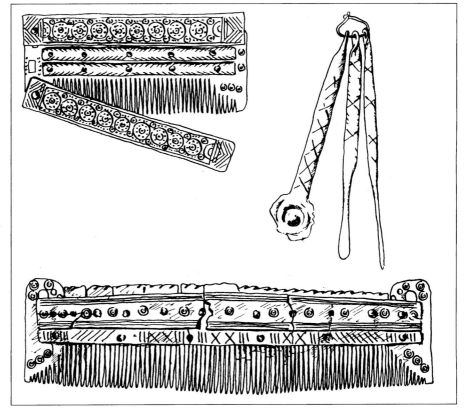

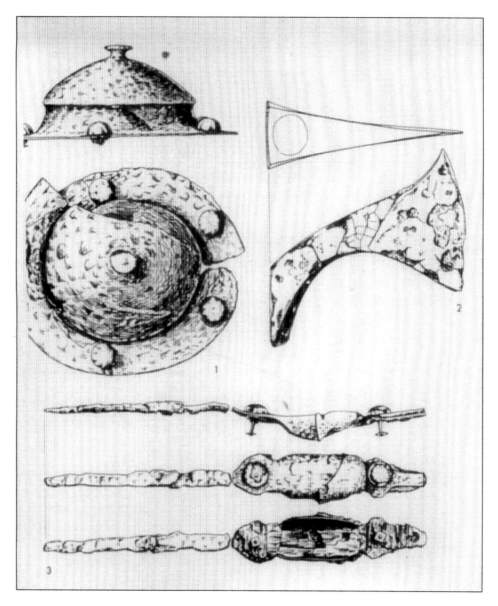

some time while negotiations were conducted with the Imperial officials for their admittance into the Empire as allies. During this time, the men would have spent most of their time in pursuit of food, but for the most part this would have been a fruitless task since any game would soon have been exhausted and even fodder for the animals would have required ever wider ranging foraging parties thus exacerbating the situation.

Skirmishes and siege warfare

The situation did not improve on the Roman side of the Danube. Food remained scarce, and the Goths became vulnerable to corrupt Roma officials who deliberately kept supplies away t drive up prices. Our man, with little to ea nothing to do and nothing to lose, was probabl among those who Ammianus says 'grumbled tha the only way out of their pressing troubles was t break their agreement [with the Romans]'. Whe the Romans killed some men of Fritigern an Alavivus' *comitatus* in AD 377, the Goths took u arms. Our man gained his first taste of victor when the local Roman frontier forces wer defeated outside Marcianople. More importantly he now had a chance to properly equip himsel

This impressive array of grave goods was buried together with a 6th-century Frankish nobleman near Krefeld-Gellep. (Museum Burg Linn, Krefeld)

Ammianus says that after their victory the Goths 'armed themselves with Roman weapons and roamed at large unresisted'. Now, with two battles under his belt and probably owning a sword, shield, several spears and perhaps a helmet, he could consider himself a fully fledged warrior. Having no family ties, he has probably attached himself to the retinue of one of the greater warriors like Fritigern.

The Goths now moved south towards Adrianople. Travelling through the settled land of Thrace, supplies were now less of a problem and the warriors were probably able to secure booty, slaves and horses as they ranged through the countryside. They met no opposition; instead their numbers were swelled by a Gothic unit in the Roman army which quickly switched allegiance. On reaching Adrianople, Fritigern's followers attempted to lay siege but, typically, were unsuccessful:

'Their attacks on the city were disorderly and unconcentrated. They lost some men of outstanding valour whom they were unable to avenge, and arrows and sling-stones accounted for many of them. Fritigern realised that it was pointless for men without experience of siege works to fight at such a disadvantage. He suggested that the siege should be abandoned and a sufficient force left behind to contain the enemy. He had no quarrel, he said, with stone walls, and he advised them to attack and pillage in perfect safety the fruitful regions which were still unguarded.' (Ammianus Marcellinus)

Thus Fritigern avoided the trap that would have destroyed his campaign. After one quick try to take a city which would have yielded him tremendous booty, he had to move on or risk exhausting the supplies in the area and the breaking up of his warband by bored young men striking out under more aggressive leaders. The warriors 'approved of this plan and advanced cautiously in small parties over the whole of Thrace. Some of their prisoners, or others who had surrendered voluntarily, pointed out to them rich districts, particularly those where food was said to be abundant.'

Logistics dictated the conduct of the campaign. Without a commissariat and organised supply system, the army had to divide up into small

The magnificent gilded spangenhelm *from the Krefeld-Gellep find. It is lined with leather and originally had a mail neck-guard, which is now rusted. (Museum Burg Linn, Krefeld)*

groups and continue moving in search of food. A large concentration or a halt for any great length of time would have destroyed them, unless an arrangement could be worked out with the Romans that would allow them to settle somewhere permanently and to draw on that region's resources. Just as defeat by the Huns had caused men like our warrior to desert Athanaric, the smell of success and a chance for booty caused others to flock to Fritigern's standard. Fritigern was now followed by: the Tervingi who had crossed the Danube with him; a band of Greuthungi – another Gothic clan; the Roman Gothic unit which had deserted to him; escaped slaves and even some Romans 'who were unable to bear the heavy burden of taxation'. The Romans, we are told by Ammianus 'were warmly welcomed and proved to be of great service as they traversed this strange country by directing

them to concealed stores of grain and hidde corners where people had taken refuge'. It wa this multi-racial group that eventual coalesced int what in later years would be called the Visigoths.

Major battles

As the Goths ranged through Thrace, the Roman gathered forces to oppose them. Eventually tw Armenian Legions trapped a large group of Goth in a mountainous defile. The Romans reinforce and knowing that the Goths could not remain i one place for long, waited at a distance for them to break camp. hoping to catch them on the mov The Goths tried to wait it out, but in the en were forced to offer battle. They sent out a ca for help from 'the raiding parties scattered in th vicinity. These obeyed the orders of their chie and returned like lightning to what they call the wagon-fort.' (Ammianus Marcellinus). Up to th point our warrior's main experience of th campaign had been riding around the countrysid picking up booty, interspersed with a few ski mishes and an assault on a fortified town. Now h would, for the first time, face a Roman field arm in formal battle.

The Battle of Ad Salices, as it became know was a bloody all-day affair in which, although th Romans suffered higher casualties, neither sid gained the upper hand. Although they ha perhaps achieved a marginal victory on the ba tlefield, the Goths were now in a very difficu position. They remained trapped in a confine area without supplies, 'all the necessities of li having been removed to fortified towns, none which the barbarians even then attempted besiege, owing to their total ignorance of oper ations of this kind'. The Roman attempt to star them out failed, however, since although sever early attempts to break out were beaten back, a alliance with a group of Huns and Alans tippe the balance in the Goths' favour and the Roman withdrew. With mobility restored, the campaig again reverted to small bands of Goths rangin through Thrace in search of supplies and plunde On one occasion some Goths caught a sma Roman infantry force at Dibaltum, and in a fore shadowing of what was to come, encircled it wi cavalry and destroyed it. On another occasio however, the Romans had the upper hand and managed to defeat a mixed band of Goths and Taifals (another east Germanic people).

While being scattered in small bands allowed Fritigern's followers to keep themselves supplied, it posed tactical problems as the main Imperial armies drew near in AD 378. When one band was ambushed and wiped out by a Roman advance force, Fritigern, worried that the separated parties would be defeated piecemeal, called his forces together in an open area where food was plentiful. For some time the Goths and Romans sparred with each other. Fritigern detached a strong force to cut the Roman supply lines, but the Goths' movements were detected by Roman scouts and blocked by a force of foot archers and cavalry. Contrary to what the Romans considered normal Germanic custom, Ammianus tells us that Fritigern moved with caution. We can imagine the main body of Goths moving slowly with their wagons, women, children, slaves and booty. Small groups of unattached warriors, like our man, continued to range at some distance from the main group. These men, probably mounted on horses, would continue to gather supplies and booty as well as providing security for the rest of the army.

The reckoning came on 9 August AD 378 near Adrianople. The battle is well known: the Romans attacked the wagon laager of the main Gothic force only to be hit in the flank by the Greuthungi and Alans who had been foraging in another area. The Roman emperor perished along with two thirds of his army. Now, with the spoils of the battlefield, Fritigern commanded an extremely well armed host, and their numbers were increased by more deserters from the Roman army, including some Imperial Guardsmen. But, powerful though it was, the army lacked a strategic goal, and with the first major setback it would start to break apart.

A campaign of attrition

Against Fritigern's wishes the victorious Goths launched another assault on the city of Adrianople, only to re-learn the lesson of the previous year. Following this, Fritigern regained control and the Goths 'made a rapid march to Constantinople, keeping in regular formation for

fear of surprise'. This passage from Ammianus, like his description of their march prior to the battle of Adrianople, indicates that the Goths kept a fairly good march discipline. This might be indicative of Fritigern's skills as a commander, or the presence of a large number of Romans in the army, or that the Goths had learned important military lessons during their long marches through Thrace. Of course there was no hope of capturing the heavily fortified Constantinople, and the Goths were once again forced to resume their nomadic trek in search for supplies.

The campaign continued in this way for another four years. There were several skirmishes and, as always, the Goths were faced with the problem of having to keep moving to find food. When supplies were exhausted in Thrace, the Goths moved on to Illyricum. In battle, the Romans could not defeat them, although they were able on occasion to catch isolated bands of

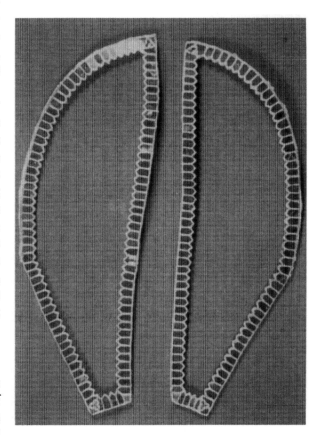

Gold and garnet saddle decoration from Krefeld-Gellep. (Museum Burg Linn, Krefeld)

Many Migration period Germanic warriors would have been mounted, like this fairly crude representation of a Thuringian. They often preferred to fight on foot, however, using their horses primarily for mobility.
(Peter Sautter, from the Hornhausen stone)

raiders. However, the Goths could never win a war of attrition.

Men like our warrior would have been very weary of tramping through the Balkans, unable to capture any cities and constantly harried by Roman troops. Many warriors had families and would have been anxious to settle down somewhere. Therefore, in AD 382, having never suffered a major defeat, the Goths asked for terms and were given land to settle and farm in return for military service: essentially the same agreement as when they had initially crossed the Danube, six years previously.

By this time our man would have been a warrior of wealth and renown. After so many successful engagements, he would probably have owned a full range of weapons, body armour and several horses. He would also have had a family and slaves. The land grant would have given him a degree of stability but he would still essentially have been a warrior. Perhaps he was one of the men whom Pactus later describes following Theodosius against the usurper Maximus:

'*There they marched under Roman leaders and Roman banners, the one time enemies of Rome, and they filled with soldiers the cities of Pannonia which*

they had not long ago emptied by hostile plundering.

In AD 395 our warrior would have been 3 years old and if he marched again wit Theodosius, this time against Eugenius, he migh have been accompanied by his son, perhaps arme with a sword his father had taken from th Adrianople battlefield. He may have been one c the many Goths who died in the bloody two-da battle at the Frigid River, prompting his son t join Alaric's revolt later in the year. If not, ou warrior would not have lived out his final years i peace. Another long, exhausting campaign i Greece and the Balkans lay in the immediat future, followed by a similar campaign in Italy culminating in the sack of Rome in AD 410. I would be another 25 years before the people wh could now properly be called the Visigoths finall established their kingdom in southern France.

THE EXPERIENCE OF BATTLE

If a protracted campaign exposed the weaknesse of the Germanic warrior, battle brought out man of his strengths. As an individual fighter he wa strong, brave and skilled in weapons handling The *Strategikon*, a 6th-century Roman militar manual, made the following observation:

'*The light-haired races place great value o freedom. They are bold and undaunted in battle Daring and impetuous as they are, they consider an timidity and even a short retreat as a disgrace. The calmly despise death as they fight violently in han to hand combat, either on horseback or on foot.*'

The tactics employed on the battlefield were no sophisticated. 'They are not interested in anythin that is at all complicated,' says the *Strategikon* their usual strategies being limited to either straightforward charge or to standing to receive a enemy attack. Complicated tactics would hav been difficult to achieve, since although the mei in the ranks had achieved a certain degree o cohesion, they were not drilled and so would no have been able to carry out complex manoeuvres Germanic tactics were not, however, entirel rimitive. As early as the 1st century AD, Tacitus ays of the Chatti (who later became part of the Frankish confederacy):

'They appoint picked men to lead them, and then bey them. They know how to keep rank, and how to recognise an opportunity – or else postpone their attack. They can map out the duties of the day and make sure the defences of the night. They know that fortune is not all to be relied on, but only valour; and – the rarest thing of all, which the gods have vouchsafed only to a military discipline like the Romans – they place more confidence in their general than in their troops. They seldom engage in swift rushes or in casual fighting – tactics which properly belong to the cavalry, with its quick successes and quick retreats. Speed suggests something like fear, whereas deliberate movement rather indicates a steady courage.'

It is only with great difficulty that we can try to build a picture of how the Germans in the Migration period engaged in combat. The greatest problem is that the two main sources, Roman historians and Germanic poets, present a stylised picture. The Romans portrayed the Germans the way the Greco-Roman world had portrayed barbarians for centuries – as wild, ill-disciplined blood-thirsty savages, in contrast to the steady, civilised Mediterranean people. Ammianus, for example, describes the Alamanni at the Battle of Strasbourg as:

'Rushing forward with more haste than caution throwing themselves on our squadrons of horse with horrible grinding of teeth and more than their usual fury. Their hair streamed behind them and a kind of madness flashed from their eyes. The Alamanni had the advantage of strength and height, the Romans of training and discipline. One side was wild and turulent, the other deliberate and cautious.'

The heroic German poems and sagas pose a different problem, since they concentrate on the deeds of a few great men, presenting battles as if they were personal duels, without giving us any idea of what happened to the mass of warriors. Although written several centuries after the Migration period, the Anglo-Saxon poem *The Battle of Maldon* gives an idea of the style preferred by the Germanic bards:

'With Wulfstan there stood two brave undaunted warriors, Aelfre and Maccus, who had no intention of making a retreat at the water-crossing, but rather they strove steadfastly against the enemy as long as they were able to wield their weapons...

'...Then one ruthless in warfare advanced, raised his weapon and his shield for protection and moved towards that man. Just as resolutely the earl went towards the commoner; each of them intended to harm the other. Then the seaman dispatched a spear of southern design so that the warriors' lord was wounded. Then he gave a thrust with the shield so

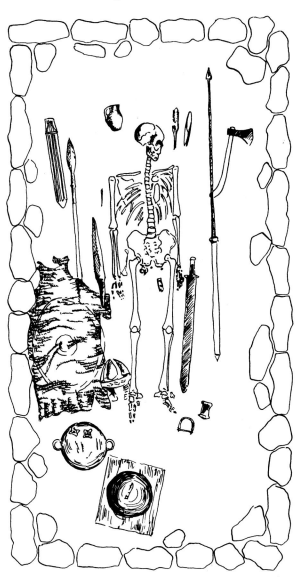

An Alamannic chieftain's grave, with the full array of weapons, including spear, sax, sword, francisca, angon, arrows, shield, mail shirt, helmet and horse furniture. (Peter Sautter, after Christlein)

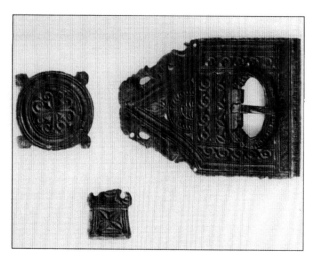

This bronze belt buckle is typical of the very wide 4th-century style. The buckle is 10.4 cm wide. Although it is of Roman origin it could easily have been worn by a Germanic warrior of the period. (Deutcher Kunstverlag, from the Praehistorische Staatssammlung, Munich)

that the shaft broke and he shattered the javelin so that it sprang out.'

The impression we get from the sources is of a very loose, individualistic style of fighting. The problem is determining how much of this is poetic licence and how much reflects reality. Archaeology provides some clues. In Tacitus' day, when the Germans fought in clan groupings, the warrior's main equipment consisted of a spear and a fairly substantial oval or rectangular wooden shield. His weaponry indicates that he fought in a fairly tight formation which is consistent with Tacitus' claim that the Chatti in his day 'knew how to keep ranks' and also with his description of a battle between Arminius and Marobodus. ('With equal expectation of victory on both sides they drew up their battle lines, not as the Germans once did, with roving assaults or in scattered bands, for they had become accustomed by lengthy military service against us to follow the standards, to support themselves with reserves and to obey the orders of commanders.')

During the Migrations the warrior's equipment changed, with throwing axes and javelins becoming more popular, and swords much more common. These weapons needed more room in a formation to be used effectively. Even more indicative is the change to a fairly small, handy, round shield with a prominent spiked boss. This type of shield would have been more useful for parrying blows in a loose formation than the larger shield of the early Germans, but would not have been as effective in providing solid protection for a close formation. The prominent boss made the shield an offensive weapon, and would have lessened its value in a closely packed formation since the rear ranks could not have exerted pressure on the front ranks without injuring them with the spiked bosses. The offensive value of these shields was noted by Ammianus: 'The barbarians (Goths) hurled themselves recklessly on our lines, dashing their shields upon the bodies of their opponents and running them through with spears and swords.'

It is probable, therefore, that tactics evolved during the Migrations, mirroring the change in Germanic armies from tribal levies to aristocratic warbands. A looser, more fluid style of warfare was more suited to the well equipped men forming the *comitatus* of a warlord. Increasingly these men rode into battle, although they remained happy fighting on foot when the situation demanded it.

Offensive formations

If we accept a fairly loose, individualistic fighting style for the Migration period Germans, the term 'formation' is perhaps something of a misnomer. None the less, the men who filled the ranks of a warlord's retinue, whether mounted or dismounted, retained a semblance of order and cohesion, even if this did not result in neat ranks and files marching in step as were seen in the armies of Rome.

The classic Germanic formation was the 'boar's head'. Adopted by the Romans and also known as the *cuneus*, it has been incorrectly translated in modern times as a 'wedge', implying a triangular formation. In fact it would be better described as an attack column. (See a full discussion on the 'wedge' in *Warrior 9, Late Roman Infantryman AD 236-565*.) The most realistic description of the boar's head comes from Tacitus, who describes the formation as 'closely compressed on all sides and secure in front, flank and rear'. This is echoed in the *Strategikon*, which says that the

Alamannic warrior, 3rd-4th century AD (See text commentary for detailed captions)

A

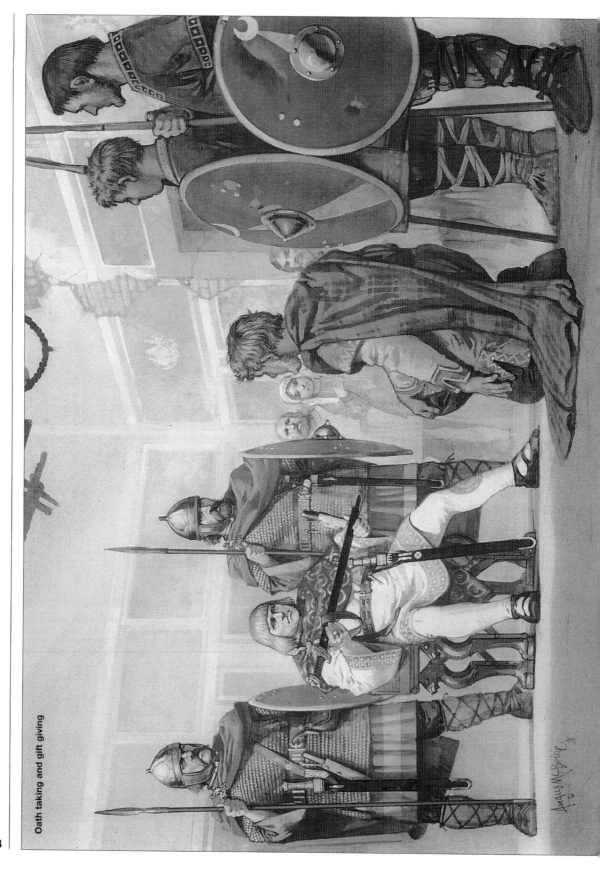

Oath taking and gift giving

B

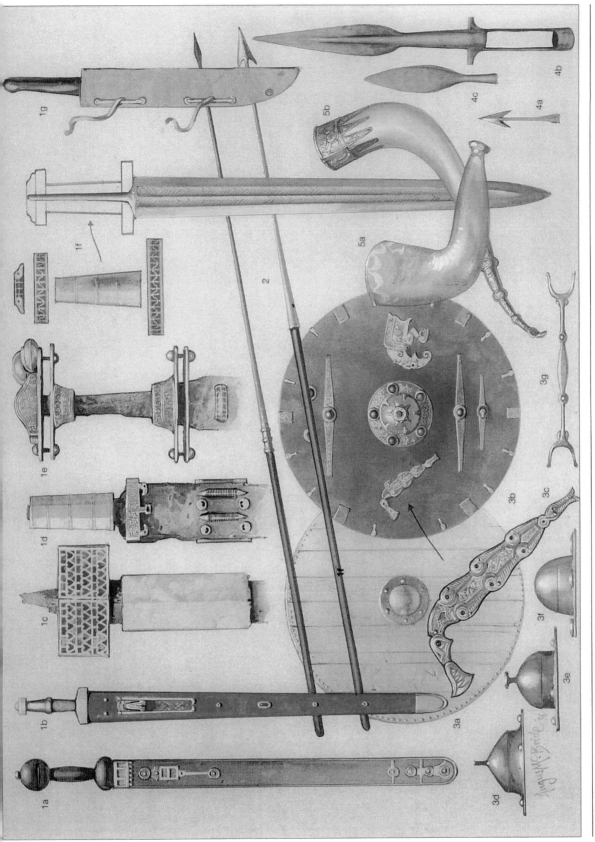

Weapons and equipment (See text commentary for detailed captions)

Augu McBride

C

Mixed cavalry/infantry action

Visigoth warrior, 5th century AD (See text commentary for detailed captions)

F

Weapons production, a Frankish workshop, 6th century

H

The Goths cross the Danube, AD 376

J

Valaris issues a challenge to personal combat

K

Frankish warrior, 6th century AD (See text commentary for detailed captions)

Angus McBride 96

L

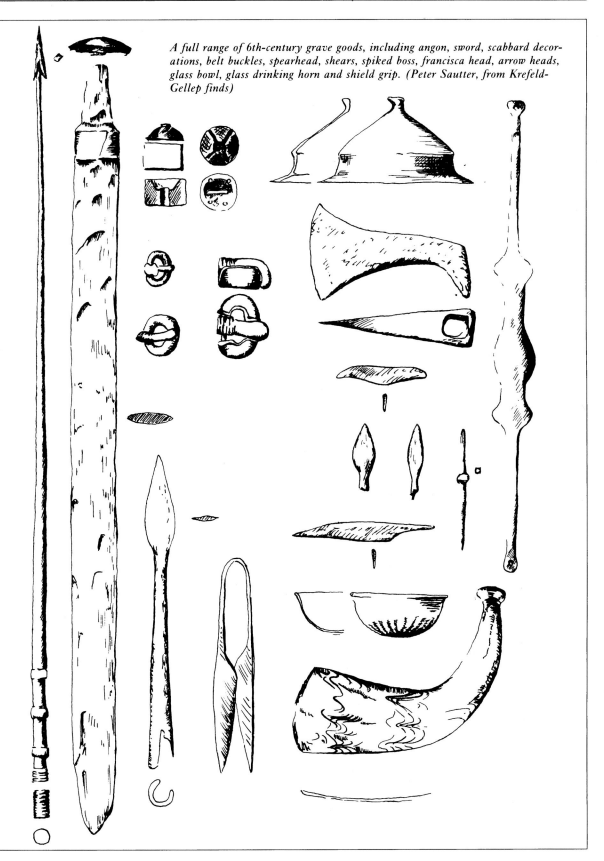

A full range of 6th-century grave goods, including angon, sword, scabbard decorations, belt buckles, spearhead, shears, spiked boss, francisca head, arrow heads, glass bowl, glass drinking horn and shield grip. (Peter Sautter, from Krefeld-Gellep finds)

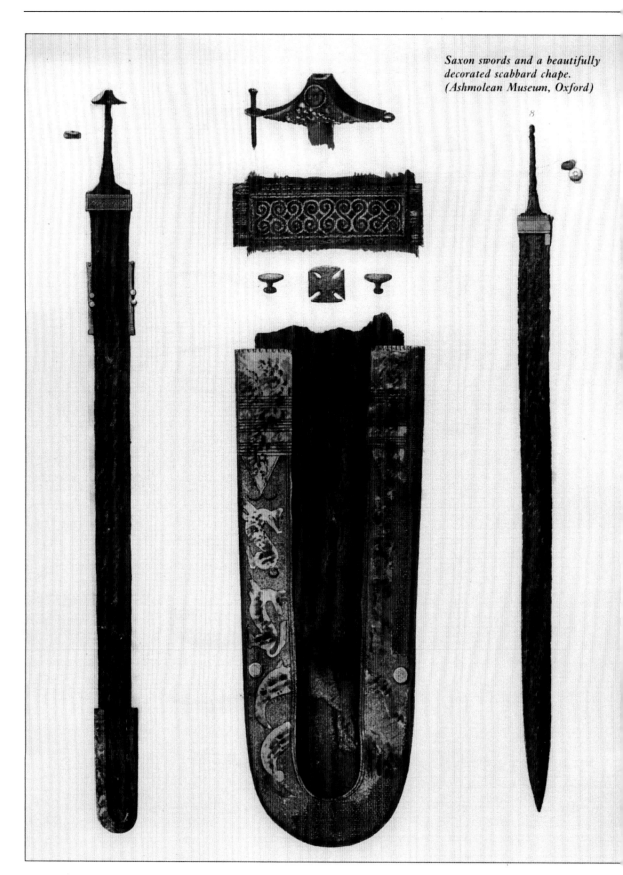

Saxon swords and a beautifully decorated scabbard chape. (Ashmolean Museum, Oxford)

Germanic peoples 'attack in formations which are as wide as they are deep'.

The boar's head was an attack formation which could be used by mounted or unmounted troops. It would be formed around the leader, with the great man taking a prominent position in the front centre and his followers taking up positions beside and behind him, according to their rank and status. The prominent warriors would occupy the front ranks, with the lesser individuals falling in behind. Ammianus said of the Goths, after the Battle of Adrianople: 'The chiefs who filled the front ranks were on fire to lay hands on Valens' ill-gotten riches, and they were closely followed by the rest, eager to be seen to share the danger of their betters.'

A good-sized *comitatus* of, say, 300 men on foot might take up a position roughly 20 men wide and 15 deep. The men in front would be well equipped veterans or men of noble blood, most of whom would probably have worn body armour and carried good swords and other prestige weapons such as angons. Further back the level of experience and quality of equipment would decrease. Serious fighting would have been conducted by the men in the front few ranks – maybe the first four. The role of those behind would have been to add weight to the charge, perhaps to support combat with overhead javelin and/or bow fire and to follow the actions of the veterans so that they would have had the necessary experience when their turn came to take up a more prominent position. Mounted men would probably have fought in shallower formations, since rear ranks would have been less able to provide support to those in front, but the principle remains the same.

The men in the formation were not drilled and would not have carried out manoeuvres to commands or signals. Rather they would have followed the movements of the leader, whose position would probably have been marked by a standard. Having a relatively narrow frontage, the boar's head would have been fairly manoeuvrable, and able to make changes of direction. The experienced men in the front would have known how to conform to the leader's movement, and the others only had to follow the men in front.

These gilded bronze animals originally decorated a Lombard warrior's shield. Towards the end of the migrations period such metallic shiled ornaments became popular throughout the Germanic world. (Deutcher Kunstverlag, from the Praehistorische Staatssammlung, Munich)

As the formation moved towards the enemy there would have been little or no attempt to maintain dressing. The *Strategikon* notes that 'either on horseback or on foot they are impetuous and undisciplined in charging, as if they were the only people in the world who are not coward's'. The leader in the centre and the men immediately around him would probably have surged forward while those on the flanks, feeling less secure, would have been inclined to hang back a bit. Just prior to contact with the enemy, therefore, the boar's head would have resembled the triangular 'wedge' of poetic descriptions.

On contact with the enemy, the formation would either have punched through or been halted. In the latter case, the boar's head would probably have flattened out as men from the rear ranks spread out to the flanks and the two lines would have become locked in combat.

The heads of a Frankish barbed javelin, spear and francisca. (Museum Burg Linn, Krefeld)

This would result in a situation like that described by Ammianus at the Battle of Adrianople when 'the opposing lines came into collision like ships of war and pushed each other to and fro, heaving under the reciprocal motion like the waves of the sea'.

Defensive formations

The impression we get from Roman writers is that the Germans greatly preferred to implement offensive tactics. However, if faced by a superior force, they could adapt and did occasionally take up defensive positions, adopting what was called a 'shieldwall'. If the offensive boar's head was well suited to manoeuvre and its ability to concentrate force, the shieldwall was designed for steadiness and greater protection. The men would form up in a tightly compressed group, shoulder to shoulder with the warriors' shields overlapping. This could be linear, several ranks deep, o perhaps facing out in all directions.

Towards the end of the Migration period and beyond, shields became larger and the spiked boss eventually became irrelevant and fell out of use. This may indicate a gradual move towards more defensive tactics, at least on the part of those warriors who usually had to fight on foot.

Later Anglo-Saxon poetry gives a brief glimpse of how a shieldwall might have been ordered:

'*Then Byrhtnoth began to place the men in array there; he rode about and gave instructions, taught the soldiers how they were to stand and maintain their position, and urged them that they should hold their shields properly, securely with their fists, and that they should not feel scared at all. When he had suitably placed the army in array he then dismounted among the people where it pleased him best to be where he knew his troop of household retainers to be most loyal.*

'*There confronting the fierce foe, Byrhtnoth stood ready with his men. He ordered the army to form the defensive barrier with shields [scildburh] and to hold teadfastly against their enemies.'* (The Battle of Maldon, AD 991).

Any attempt to move by the undrilled warriors who formed a shieldwall would have caused the formation to lose alignment and cohesion since the warriors moved forward as individuals at different rates, allowing dangerous gaps to appear. If a commander needed to move his men to a new defensive position he would have to take the chance of breaking out of the formation, moving forward with disordered groups and then re-forming at the new position. This apparently is what Byrhtnoth did at Maldon. Such a manoeuvre would have been extremely risky, since the disordered formation could easily have been swept aside by an ordered one. Byrhtnoth got away with it because he had a body of water separating his men from the enemy.

Another defensive tactic used by the eastern Germans was to form up behind a wagon laager. No doubt this was adopted from the Asiatic Steppe peoples, who continued to use wagon laagers for many centuries. Ammianus records the Goths at Adrianople, for example, forming defensively behind wagons 'which were drawn up in a regular circle'.

Presumably the warriors defending a wagon laager would have been primarily armed with missile weapons, with the aim of preventing an enemy from coming to close quarters.

Cavalry actions

The Germanic fighting man of the Migrations was neither an infantryman nor a cavalryman: he was an all-round warrior with a full range of fighting skills who fought as an individual in a loosely defined 'unit'. The German historian Hans Delbrueck effectively sums up the situation:

'For the Germans who had settled among the Romans, the cavalry was necessarily the arm to which they devoted all their care and attention, not in the specifically cavalry-related sense, but in the sense of the man who moves into the field on horseback knows how to control his horse and to fight from his mounted position, but is also ready, if the circumstances call for it, to dismount and fight on foot. The warrior was not so much a cavalryman as

a man on horseback; expressed in another way, he was a cavalryman for the reason that he could do everything in conjunction with his mounted situation. This period was not capable of forming tactical units. The whole military system was based on the individual, the person. The man who can only fight on foot with a close-combat weapon is very insignificant if he is not a member of a tactical unit, while the man who fights on foot with bow and arrow can only provide a support weapon. The man who fights on horseback is superior to both as an individual combatant.'

The *Strategikon* notes: 'If they [the Germans] are hard pressed in cavalry actions, they dismount at a pre-arranged sign and line up on foot,' and there are many examples of this occurring throughout the period. At Strasbourg in AD 357 Ammianus says that the mounted Alamannic nobles dismounted and joined the men on foot; and at Taginae in AD 552 we learn that 'in the middle of the phalanx, Narses placed the Lombards, Heruls, and other barbarians and had them dismount'. (Procopius)

The reason given by both Ammianus and Procopius for dismounting was to prevent a hasty

This mounted warrior might be a Lombard, or someone in the service of the Byzantine army. The lamellar armour and two-handed use of the lance originated on the Steppes and became popular in the 6th-and 7th-centuries. (Peter Sautter, from the Isola Rizza dish)

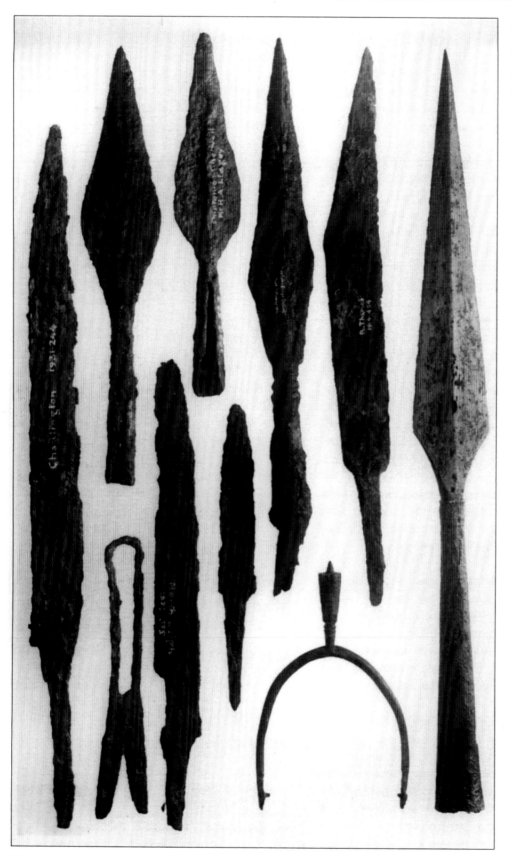

A selection of Anglo Saxon grave goods, including several spearheads, saxes, a spur and a set of shears. (Ashmolean Museum, Oxford)

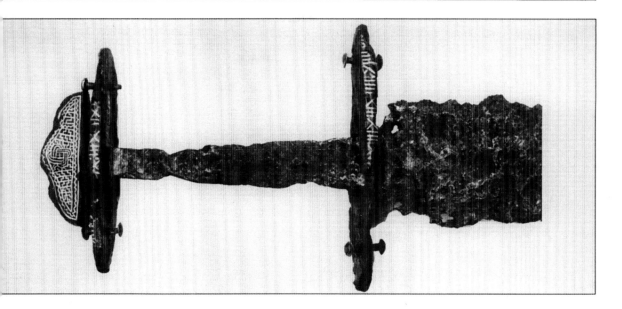

A 7th-century sword hilt decorated in silver and brass. (Deutcher Kunstverlag, from the Praehistorische Staatssammlung, Munich)

etreat. This is highly unlikely. These Roman authors had not understood that the Germanic warrior, even if on horseback, was perhaps closer to a mounted infantryman than a cavalryman. When fighting on the defensive, he would nearly always dismount and he might even do the same when attacking. At the Battle of Mount Vesuvius in AD 553: 'The Goths had driven their own horses away and were all drawn up on foot, their front facing the enemy, in a deep phalanx. When the Romans saw that, they likewise dismounted and took up the same formation.'

Steady men on foot in a stationary shieldwall had little to fear from a cavalry attack. In a skirmish prior to the Battle of Taginae, Procopius vividly describes the failure of a Gothic cavalry attack on a small Roman infantry detachment, which leaves no doubt as to why the Germans preferred fighting on foot:

'The cavalry charged upon them with much noise and shouting in order to overrun them in their first assault; but the 50 men shield to shield in close formation awaited the attack that the Goths, getting in each other's way in their rush, now attempted. The wall of shields and spears of the 50 men was so thick and tight that it brilliantly repulsed the attack. At the same time, with their shields they made a great noise, scaring the horses while their riders recoiled from the spear points. The horses, which became wild as a result of the close quarters and the noise of the shields, and could move neither forward nor

backward, reared up, and the riders could do nothing against this tightly formed band that neither wavered nor yielded, while they vainly spurred their horses on against them.'

It would be wrong to assume, however, that the Germanic warrior always dismounted to fight. He probably preferred to fight mounted if pursuing a broken opponent or exploiting a sudden advantage like the famous Gothic cavalry charge on the Roman flank at Adrianople. Many small skirmishes were most likely fought between roving bands of mounted men. Eastern Germanic tribes like the Ostrogoths and Gepids, who migrated from the Steppes, were perhaps more inclined to fight mounted than their western cousins from the forests of Germania, but neither case was absolute.

When fighting mounted, the Germanic warrior's tactics did not vary from his offensive tactics on foot. He would form up opposite his enemy, then launch a straightforward charge. The *Strategikon* hints that the Romans adopted some of their cavalry tactics from the Germans when it recommends that Roman cavalry should 'lean forward, cover their heads with their shields, hold their lances high as their shoulders in the manner of the fair haired races, and protected by their shields they ride in good order, not too fast but at

This 6th-century mosaic from Carthage depicts a Vandal or Alan. His loose tunic and trousers with their decorative bands are typical 6th-century Germanic dress. (British Museum, London)

a trot, to avoid having the impetus of their charge breaking up their ranks before coming to blows with the enemy, which is a real risk'.

It is quite probable, however, that the Germanic charge was less controlled. At Taginae, for example, Procopius says: 'The Gothic cavalry, leaving their infantry far behind them, charged out wildly with blind trust in the weight of their lances, and when they encountered the enemy, they reaped the fruits of their thoughtless charge.'

THE PLATES

A: Alamannic warrior, 3rd-4th century AD

This warrior, from the beginning of the Germanic Migrations, is representative of those men who were among the first to settle on the Roman side of the upper Rhine. He might have fought in the campaigns of Chnodomar in the mid-4th century, which culminated in the defeat at Argentoratum (Strasbourg). His dress and equipment are mostly of native manufacture, showing little Roman

influence. After campaigning in Gaul, and with initial successes against Roman troops, he would have gradually changed his appearance, adding weapons, armour and clothing of Roman manufacture. By the time of the Battle of Strasbourg he would have been barely distinguishable from his Roman opponents (many or most of whom would have been Franks or Alamanni themselves).

His arms and equipment are typical of a well equipped warrior in a chieftain's *comitatus* along the Rhine frontier. A Burgundian or Frank would not have looked very different. His main weapon is a spear, backed up with a *francisca* (throwing axe), a sword and a fairly small, handy shield with a spiked boss. His fine sword, an example of which was found in an Alamannic grave, would be a family heirloom which he would no doubt pass down to his son. Because of their expense, many lesser warriors might have had to go without a sword until they could capture one on the battlefield or perhaps be given one by their chieftain (see Plate B). The shield, with its spiked iron boss, is as much an offensive as a defensive weapon, allowing its owner to deliver an incapacitating punch to an opponent. We do not know how the Germans decorated their shields, but Tacitus says they were brightly painted. Roman depictions in earlier periods, and shields of Germanic auxiliaries in the Roman army, indicate that combinations of stars and crescent moons vere extremely popular. The bolt heads holding he rear hand grip were often made part of the lecoration, and in the 6th century some shields vere adorned with gilded metal plates of warriors and mythical beasts.

Prior to the Migrations, many German warriors vore their hair tied in a distinctive knot (*A1*). Although the style was widespread, it was particuarly favoured by the Swabians (Suevi, or Suebi) and it is known to us today as the 'Swabian knot'. We have no way of knowing if the style continued nto the Migrations period, but it is quite possible hat some Alamanni, who are closely related to the Swabians, wore their hair in this style in the early years. Sidonius Apollinaris compares the 5th century Franks to monsters 'on the crown of whose pates lies the hair that has been drawn oward the front, while the neck, exposed by the oss of its covering, shows bright'. This might ndicate a continuation of this hairstyle.

The *francisca* (*A2*) was widely used by most western German peoples during the Migrations, especially the Franks and Alamanni. Although some accounts mention it being thrown at the enemy just prior to contact, many others speak of hand axes being used in close-quarter fighting, and they may have been used by poorer warriors as a substitute for a sword.

Despite the fairly popular idea that archery does not fit with the 'heroic' image of the German warrior, many Alamannic warriors were probably equipped as archers. In Alamannic graves poorer men were usually buried with their equipment; arrows, a knife and perhaps a *francisca*. Bows and arrows have also been found in north German bog deposits, and literary evidence shows that the Goths and Lombards also employed large numbers of archers. The Germanic bow (*A3*) was a wooden longbow.

The Romans portrayed the Germans as wild savages, and this image has remained. A look at the detailed craftsmanship of some of their posessions, like the brooches at *A4*, shows that while they may have been behind the Romans in enginering and political organisation, they were far from being a primitive unskilled people. These brooches are typically Alamannic, although they hare features common to most Germanic styles.

The brooch in the shape of a fish is less common than the other styles, and may have belonged to a Christian convert.

The helmet at *A5*, although pre-dating the Migrations, gives us an idea as to how German warriors decorated captured Roman equipment to suit their own tastes. It started out as a Roman legionary helmet from the 1st century, which probably fell into German hands as battlefield salvage. The cheek pieces and neck guard were removed by the new owner (perhaps they were damaged, or perhaps he preferred to sacrifice protection for comfort), and the ear holes were welded over, leaving only a simple iron bowl. This was then lined with leather and decorated with feathers and animal skin – probably marten. The decoration may have been thought to have totemic protective powers similar to the wild boar crests frequently referred to in the poem *Beowulf*.

B: Oath taking and gift giving

This scene depicts a young nobleman with several of his own followers who have crossed from the east of the Rhine to take service with a powerful Burgundian chieftain who has established himself on Roman territory. The *comitatus* of a Migration period warlord was usually made up of adventurous young men from several tribes; loyalty was

A fragment of Frankish lamellar armour. Although this find was too badly rusted to reconstruct, some Alamannic lamellar has been – see Plate L. (Museum Burg Linn, Krefeld)

more man to man, and not based on national origins. Entering a lord's service was marked by taking oaths of loyalty, which were cemented by the presentation of gifts. Because of his noble ancestry and the followers he has brought with him, this young man is being presented with a valuable sword from his new lord. The sword,

This large silver and enamel brooch is typical of the migration period. (Deutcher Kunstverlag, from the Praehistorische Staatssammlung, Munich)

with its interlocking rings on the hilt, symbolise the bond between the leader and the follower: the young man leaves the lord's service, or if he killed, the sword will most likely be returned unless it is given as a permanent gift in return fo exceptional service.

From the laws of the Visigoths we gain som insight into the legal aspects of gift giving and th web of obligations this implied:

'If anyone gives arms to a buccellarius [warrior i a retinue] or grants him something, and if he remain in allegiance to his patron, that which was give would remain in his possession. If he selects anothe patron for himself, he would have the freedom t commit himself to anyone he wished since a free ma cannot be restrained because he is under his ow power. But he should return everything to the patro he left. A similar procedure should be observed r regard to the sons of a patron or a buccellarius. If th son wanted to pledge allegiance, he would get pos session of his donations. If they believe that the ought to leave the service of the patron's sons o grandsons, they would return everything that wa given to their parents by the patron. And whatever buccellarius acquires under a patron, half of it woul be under the control of the patron or his sons. Th buccellarius who acquired it would possess the othe half. And if he leaves a daughter, we decree that sh remain under the control of the patron. Neverthele. we also decree that the patron should provide for he a man of equal status who can marry her. But if sh perhaps chooses for herself another man against th wish of the patron, she should restore to the patron o his heirs whatever was given to her father by th patron or the parents of the patron.'

C: Weapons and equipment
C1: Blade Weapons. The sword was th Germanic warrior's ultimate weapon. It was time consuming and costly to produce, and therefore finely crafted sword would have been a statu symbol as well as a weapon. While some swords like *C1a* from the Thorsberg bog deposit, ma have been of Roman origin, many high qualit blades were produced throughout the Germa world. *C1b* is a 5th-century Gothic sword from Russia. The magnificent sword at *C1c*, althoug found near the Rhine in Alamannic territory, wa

probably brought west by one of Attila's followers. Its wide hand-guard and gold and garnet decoration is an east German style, originating on the Steppes. The style was later widely copied in the west and became an almost universal Germanic aristocratic style. *C1d* was probably made by a Franco-Roman smith in the region of Namur, and is more typical of 4th-5th-century styles. The 6th-century Lombard 'ring sword' at *C1e* is an example of a style that became increasingly popular towards the end of the period. It may be that the interlocking rings on the pommel represent the oaths of loyalty binding a warrior to his lord. Better quality German swords had pattern welded blades (*C1f*). These were made by iron rods twisted together, hammered, cut up and then recombined. The reconstructed hilt is based on that found in the grave of the Frankish King Childeric. *C1g* shows a fairly simple Lombard *Sax*. These long knives were almost universal throughout the Germanic world and would have been multi-purpose tools as well as serving as secondary weapons.

C2: Angons. These were probably prestige weapons which could be used by well equipped warriors in most western German armies from the 3rd to the 6th-century. They are very similar in appearance to the old Roman pila which were beginning to fall out of use in the Roman army at this time. The 6th-century writer Agathius describes their use by Franks in some detail:

'The Angons are spears which are neither very short nor very long; they can be used, if necessary, for throwing like a javelin, and also in hand to hand combat. The greater part of the angon is covered with iron and very little wood is exposed. In battle the Frank throws the angon, and if it hits an enemy, the spear is caught in the man and neither the wounded man nor anyone else can draw it out. The barbs hold inside the flesh, causing great pain, and in this way a man whose wound may not be in a vital spot dies. If the angon strikes a shield, it is fixed there, hanging down with the butt on the ground. The angon cannot be pulled out because the barbs have penetrated the shield, nor can it be cut off with a sword because the wood of the shaft is covered with iron. When the Frank sees the situation, he quickly puts his foot on the butt of the spear, pulling down, and the man

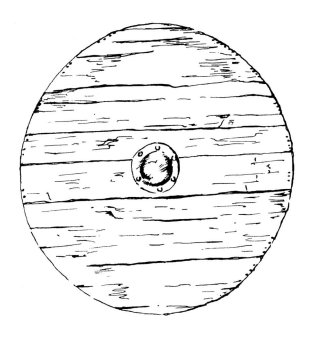

This shield from northern Germany is made up of wooden planks bound with leather. It is about a metre in diameter with a round iron boss – a style more common before and after the Migrations, which may indicate a more static fighting style than the prominent spiked bosses which were popular during the height of the Migrations.

holding it falls leaving his head and chest unprotected. The unprotected warrior is then killed either by a stroke of the axe or a thrust with another spear.'

C3: The Germanic warrior's main defensive equipment was his shield. *C3a* is the remains of a north German shield from the start of this period while *C3b* is a reconstruction of the Angle shield from Sutton Hoo. Metal decorations like those on the Sutton Hoo shield were in fashion in the 6th-7th-centuries throughout the Germanic world. Mythical beasts like the dragon at *C3c* were common. *C3d-f* show a selection of Germanic shield bosses. *C3d* is a 4th-century Alamanic spiked boss, *C3e* is 6th-century Frankish, and *C3f* is a 6th-century rounded Lombard boss. The rounded style was more common amongst the Romans or Romanised Germans and may indicate a static style of fighting, allowing rear ranks to push forward on the front ranks with their shields, something that would have been difficult to do with the spiked versions which were more suited to an individualistic fighting style. The

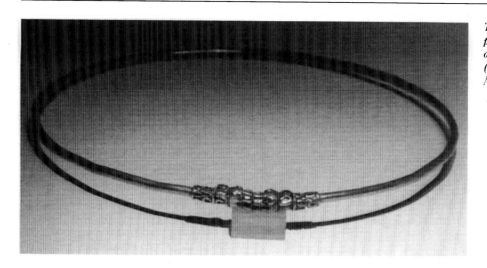

shield was held by a single hand grip (*C3g*) which was bolted on behind the boss.

C4: Most German warriors carried a variety of spears and javelins. *C4a* is a typical javelin head, *C4b* is the head of a Frankish hunting spear; and *C4c* shows a conventional spearhead. Many German spears also would have had bronze butt-spikes. Not all the warrior's time was spent in action. Feasting formed just as much a part of his life as campaigning and drinking horns such as those depicted at *C5* would have been an essential part of the aristocratic warrior's equipment. *C5a* is a glass Frankish horn; *C5b* is a decorated Angle auroch's horn.

D: Mixed cavalry/infantry action

The early Germans were noted by Tacitus for the practice of mixing light infantry with cavalry:

'Generally speaking, their strength lies in infantry rather than cavalry. So foot soldiers accompany the cavalry into action, their speed of foot being such that they can easily keep up with the charging horsemen. The best men are chosen from the whole body of young warriors and placed with the cavalry in front of the main battle line.'

This practice appears to have continued into the Migration period, since prior to the Battle of Strasbourg, in AD 357, Ammianus Marcellinus states that the Alamannic cavalry were 'interspersed with light-armed foot, whose use was dictated by considerations of safety. They knew that for all his skill a mounted warrior meeting with one of our cataphracts, and using one hand

to hold his reins and shield and the other to brandish a spear, could inflict no harm on an opponent dressed in mail, whereas in the heat of the fight, when a man is occupied solely with the danger that stares him in the face, someone on foot, creeping along unnoticed close to the ground, can stab the horse in the flank, bring his rider headlong to the ground, and finish him off without difficulty.'

Divisions between cavalry and infantry were probably not that clear-cut in Germanic armies, and it is unlikely that mounted troops were thought of as a separate arm on the battlefield. Men on horse were quite happy dismounting to fight on foot and foot soldiers would mount up if they captured horses. It could be that mixing mounted and dismounted men was less of a deliberate tactic and more a result of individual decisions made by the warriors as to whether or not to remain mounted to fight. In a defensive, set-piece battle, mounted men probably dismounted, as the Alamanni did at Strasbourg and the Lombards and Heruls did at Taginae. In a more fluid engagement, men who owned horses might remain mounted while those who did not might fight alongside on foot.

E: Treatment of the wounded

Medical treatment was not one of the strong points of Germanic armies. Some might have been lucky enough to recruit Roman surgeons, but for the most part care of the wounded was an *ad hoc* arrangement. Tacitus tells us that in the 1st century the warrior was dependent on his family for care if he was wounded:

'*Close by them are their nearest and dearest, so that they can hear the shrieks of their women and wailing of their children. These are the witnesses whom each man reverences most highly, whose praise he most desires. It is to their mothers and wives that they go to have their wounds treated, and the women are not afraid to compare gashes. They also carry supplies of food to the combatants and encourage them.*' Tacitus also mentions that the Germans would '*bring back the bodies of the fallen even when a battle hangs in the balance*'.

During an actual migration, the warriors would have had their families close by, and it is highly likely that the women, children and infirm would have been expected to lend a hand. A warrior wounded on a raid far from his home territory would not have had the benefit of being looked after by his family, however, and would have had to rely on whatever treatment he himself or his comrades could perform.

F: Visigoth warrior, 5th century AD

This man, who may have crossed the Danube as a baby in AD 376, is one of the followers of Alaric, who sacked Rome in AD 410. He has lived all or most of his life within the Roman Empire, and he has fought both for and against Roman armies. Consequently most of his equipment is of Roman origin. His helmet is a typical Roman 4th-5th-century style, with a central ridge holding together the two-part bowl. Separate cheek and neck guards are laced on to the main bowl. Although he has not yet managed to acquire body armour, many of his comrades would have. Although the Visigoths seem to have usually fought on foot in formal battle, most would have acquired horses for mobility on campaign.

The Germanic warriors favoured brightly dyed clothing, and green with scarlet trim is mentioned in several sources as being worn by Goths and Franks. *F1a:* This *spangenhelm*-style helmet is more traditionally associated with the Goths. Although the general style of it probably originated on the Danube among the Sarmatians, this version was probably made in a Mediterranean workshop and could have been worn by soldiers of any nationality in the 5th and 6th centuries.

Spangenhelm were characterised by a multi-part bowl constructed of four or six panels held together by reinforcement bands. Separate nose, cheek and neck guards were usually added. Neck guards were frequently of link-mail.

F1b: This simple helmet is similarly constructed to the one worn by the main figure. It comes from southern France, where the Visigoths settled in

Belts became narrower towards the end of the migrations period. These 7th-century fittings, typically decorated in silver and brass are 5.8 cm at the widest point. (Deutcher Kunstverlag, from the Praehistorische Staatssammlung, Munich)

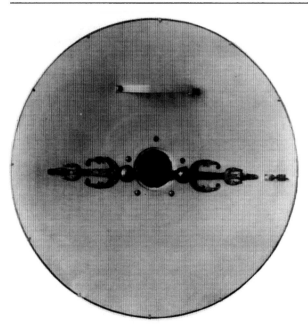

The Gerrmanic Warrior held his shield by a single grip behind the central boss as can be seen in this reconstruction of the Sutton Hoo shield. The arm strap to the side is unlikely as it would have prevented the warrior from giving an offensive punch with the shield. (British Museum, London)

the 5th-century, and may represent a continuation of Roman construction methods in Visigoth workshops. *F2a:* Is an example of the wide utility belt worn by Romans and Germans in the 4th-5th centuries. Some examples are as wide as 10cm. The buckles and strap attachments could be used to attach a purse (*F2c*), knife, fire-steel (*F2d*) and any other items the warrior might find useful. Several examples have a buckle facing upwards, indicating that they were worn with a supporting shoulder strap like a modern British Sam Browne. Swords could be worn from a baldric or from a secondary waist belt like the main figure. *F2b:* This shows a narrower style of belt worn in the 6th-century. The buckles and metal work are decorated with gold and silver wire. The purse at the back (*F2c*) is from the Sutton Hoo find. *F2e* shows 4th-century bronze belt fittings from the middle Rhine which could have been worn by a Frankish warrior or a Roman soldier. *F2f* is a 5th-century Gothic belt buckle from Southern Russia. This gives us an idea of the styles that might have been worn by Goths who had less contact with the Romans. The style is thought by some archae-

ologists to be typical of the Gepids, another east German people who were in frequent conflict with the Goths. It has the same eagle-head design as the Alamannic brooch (*A4*), suggesting similarities between the widespread Germanic cultures in this period of mass movement of peoples.

A selection of Visigoth brooches are depicted (*F3*). The eagle Brooch (*F3a*) comes from Visigothic Spain but very similar brooches have been attributed to Ostrogothic Italy, perhaps indicating a common Gothic style. *F3b* is a Visigothic version of the common Germanic radiate style while the more simple bow brooch (*F3c*) is a Roman style that remained widespread in Italy.

G: Weapons production, a Frankish workshop 6th century

The Germanic smiths were held in very high regard by their people due to the importance of their craft. A 6th-century Frankish smith, for example, was buried with the tools of his trade together with a spear, sword, axe, long knife and a purse containing 17 silver coins. Similar finds occur among the Gepids and Lombards.

This scene shows weapons production in a Frankish workshop with a master smith supervising several apprentices. They are working on making a pattern-welded blade. This technique involved twisting iron rods together then hammering them out to form a solid core. The finished blade would display a shimmering, almost lifelike, pattern where the rods had melded together. The proud owners of such weapons would give them names and imbue them with heroic characteristics.

H: Feasting, a chieftain's great hall

Communal feasting in the company of his comrades was an integral part of the warrior's life. The great hall was the home to all the warriors of a warlord's *comitatus*, and after the meal benches and tables would be cleared away to give the men a place to sleep. This feasting and drinking played an important part in forming and strengthening the bonds between the fighting men of the warband. Men who ate, drank and amused themselves together would know each other's strength and weaknesses when it came time to stand side by side on the battlefield. Important occasions were always marked by a feast, and at such times the chieftain would reward his followers with gifts such as arm rings, clothing and weapons. The poem *Beowulf* gives many colourful descriptions of such feasting:

'Orders were immediately given for the decoration of the interior of Heorot, and a large number of men and women made the banqueting hall ready. Golden tapestries gleamed along the walls and there were many wonderful objects to be seen...

'...A bench was cleared, so the Geats could sit together in the banqueting hall. There in the pride of their strength, those bold fighting men took their seats. A servant who carried an ornamental ale-cup performed the office of pouring out the sparkling beer. From time to time a clear voiced poet sang...

'...Laughter and a cheerful din resounded from the soldiers as they talked merrily. Wealhtheow, Hrothgar's queen, now made her appearance according to courtly custom. The noble lady first presented a goblet to Hrothgar. She begged him to enjoy the revels, upon which the king gladly took part in the eating and drinking...

'...As often before, a great company bivouacked in the hall. Benches were cleared away and pillows and bedding spread upon the floor.'

I: The Goths cross the Danube, AD 376

During the migratory period there were many epic movements of people from one corner of Europe to another: the Vandals and Alans from Germany through France and Spain to Africa; the Angles and Saxons to Britain; and the Ostrogoths and later the Lombards into Italy. But it was the crossing of the Danube by the *Tervingi* and *Greuthungi* clans of Goths (later known as the Visigoths) in AD 376 which would set future patterns. The contemporary historian Ammianus Marcellinus vividly described the event:

'The work of transportation went on night and day. The Goths embarked by troops on boats and rafts and canoes made from hollowed tree-trunks. The crowd was such that many tried to swim and were drowned in the struggle against the force of the stream. The barbarians, after crossing the river, were distressed by want of food and these loathsome generals (the Roman officers in charge) devised an abominable form of barter. They collected all the dogs that their insatiable greed could find and exchanged each of them for a slave, and among these slaves were some sons of leading men.'

J: The Battle of Campus Mauriacus, AD 451

This scene shows a shieldwall of Visigoths serving in the army of Aetius standing firm in the face of an attack from mounted Ostrogoths serving Attila. Since the ancestors of the Visigoths crossed the Danube 75 years have passed and they now have a well established kingdom in southern France. Their dress, equipment and fighting methods are far closer to the Romans than to their Ostrogoth cousins who have been living on the Steppes of eastern Europe during the intervening years.

While the experience of facing a mass of charging horsemen would have been terrifying, the Visigoths have little to fear as long as they can maintain their cohesion and keep an unbroken shieldwall facing the enemy. The Ostrogoths, on the other hand, hope to cause enough panic for the enemy formation to break up, at which point all advantage would pass to the mounted men. When this fails, all they can do is throw their javelins or stab with lances as they wheel around for another try.

The Visigoths on the left wing of Aetius' army bore the brunt of the fighting and stood firm in the face of repeated attacks from both Ostrogoths and Huns.

K: Valaris issues a challenge to personal combat

Germanic society was a heroic society and much of the endemic warfare that supported it was aimed at providing the warriors with a chance to increase their reputations. Consequently, it is hardly surprising that personal challenges to combat were frequently issued to the enemy army, with man-to-man duels being fought out in front of the warriors of both sides before the general engagement began. We learn from the writings of Procopius that by the mid-6th century this custom was being followed by Germans, Huns, Romans and Persians. This plate represents one such incident during the Gothic War in Italy:

'A Goth, Valaris by name, tall of stature and most terrifying, an active man and a good fighter, rode his

These interestingly decorated strap ends adorned the eblt of a wealthy warrior at the end of the migration period. (Deutcher Kunstverlag, from the Praehistorische Staatssammlung, Munich)

horse out before the rest of the army and took his stand in the open space between the armies, clad in a corselet and wearing a helmet on his head, and challenged all the Romans, if anyone was willing to do battle with him.'

Artabazes, an Armenian in the Roman army, took up the challenge. They 'rode their horses toward each other and when they came close, both thrust their spears, but Artabazes, anticipating his opponent, delivered the first blow and pierced the right side of Valaris'. Valaris died, but his spear jammed against a rock and drove into Artabazes' neck, killing him also. (Procopius)

L: Frankish warrior, 6th century AD

This man represents one of the warriors who followed Butilin into Italy in the 550s. He is based on the earlier descriptions of Franks by Sidonius Apollinaris as well as the contents of the grave of a contemporary Frankish chieftain from Krefeld-Gellep in Germany. By this time the Franks had consolidated their rule throughout France and were extending their power into Germany and Italy. Many years of successful campaigning had provided plenty of opportunity for a capable Frankish warrior to equip himself with high quality weapons and armour.

In the 6th-7th centuries shields were commonly decorated with a combination of metal plaques and decorated bolt heads. This style seems to have been universal in the Germanic world at this time. Metal shield rims were probably less common than leather, although Sidonius Apollinaris does describe warriors of a 5th century Frankish *comitatus* carrying shields with 'silvery white rims'.

The elaborate decoration on the panels of the warrior's *spangenhelm* from Krefeld-Gellep (*L1*) suggests Italian manufacture. The helmet may have been picked up during the Italian campaign. Archaeologists have discovered 29 similar helmets spread throughout the Germanic world from Scandinavia to Italy and France to Russia (but none in the British Isles). *L2* is an Alamannic helmet and *L2b* is a Lombard front plate from a helmet of similar construction. During the 6th-century Lamellar armour of eastern origin became increasingly popular. The magnificent panoply at *L3* is from an Alamannic grave at Niederstotzingen. There are several illustrations of Lombards wearing a similar style, and fragments of lamellar armour have also been found in Frankish graves. *L3a* shows how lamellar armour was constructed by binding individual iron plates (*lamellae*) together. By the 6th-century most well equipped Frankish warriors would have ridden into battle, but they were not necessarily cavalrymen. In a fast skirmish, raid or pursuit they probably would have fought mounted, but in formal battle they still frequently dismounted to fight on foot. *L4* and *L5* show contemporary spurs and a horse bit.

GLOSSARY

A gilded 6th-century Germanic brooch. The style is unusual and probably represents mythical beasts. (Deutcher Kunstverlag, from the Praehistorische Staatssammlung, Munich)

Alamanni (*Alamannen, Alamans*): a confederation of German tribes who were one of Rome's main opponents in this period. The name means 'all people'. Their descendants are the modern Alsatians, German Swiss and the inhabitants of most of Baden.

The ancient confederacy probably included some Swabians, together with the Hermunduri and Juthungi.

Alans: Steppe nomads of either Iranian or Turkish origin who joined with many of the migrating Germans. Some joined the Visigoths, some accompanied the Vandals, and others remained outside the Empire and were absorbed by the Huns.

Anglo-Saxons: the common name given to the Germanic invaders of Britain. They included Angles, Saxons, Jutes and possibly some Frisians, Franks and Alamanni.

Ammianus: Ammianus Marcellinus. A 4th century Roman officer and historian who wrote about the wars of the Franks, Alamanni and Goths.

Angon: a spear used primarily by western Germans, which had a long iron tip. It was usually thrown just prior to contact with the enemy, and appears to have been very similar to the ancient Roman *pilum*.

Baldric: a sword-belt worn over the shoulder.

Beowulf: the hero of the 8th-century Anglo-Saxon poem which gives us much of our insight into attitudes of the Germanic warrior society.

Boar's Head: a loosely formed attack column favoured by the Germans and copied by the Romans (who called it *Cuneus*); often mistakenly thought of as a triangular wedge formation.

Buccellarius: a term used by the Visigoths for a member of a war leader's retinue.

Burgundians: a German people from the middle Rhine who moved into France, giving their name to modern Burgundy.

Cataphract: a very heavily armoured cavalryman.

Comitatus: the retinue of a Germanic war leader.

Fabricae: Roman state-controlled arms factories.

Francisca: a hatchet used as a weapon by the Migration period Germans. It was particularly common among the peoples of the Rhine frontier. It could be thrown at an opponent or retained for use as a side-arm.

Franks: a German confederacy which formed along the lower Rhine frontier and later moved into what is now the Netherlands, Belgium and France, giving their name to the latter nation. They were probably formed from the tribes of the Chamavi, Chattuarii, Batavians, Sugambri, Ubii, Tencteri, Marsi, Bructeri and Chatti.

Foederati (*federates*): foreign troops serving in the Roman army under their own leaders.

Gepids: an east German people who were often in conflict with the Goths. They remained on the steppes and became part of Attila's empire. After Attila's death they led the Germanic revolt against the Huns. They were conquered by the Avars and Lombards in the 6th century.

Goths: one of the major east Germanic peoples who moved into the Roman Empire. They became split into two quite separate groups: the **Visigoths**, who were descended from the various clans which crossed into the Roman Empire to escape the Huns in AD 376, later settling in southern France and Spain; and the **Ostrogoths**, who were descended from those Goths who remained under Hunnic control, later settling in Italy at the end of the 5th century.

Greuthungi: one of the Gothic clans which crossed the Danube in AD 376, later merging with the Tervingi and some other groups to form the Visigoths.

Illyricum: a Roman province roughly equating to the former Yugoslavia of modern times.

Lamellar armour: a form of body armour originating in the East, made up of small iron plates laced together.

Lombards (*Langobardi*): a west German tribe which played no part in the early history of the Migrations but which took advantage of the devastation of the Gothic wars to invade and occupy Italy in the late 6th century. The name means 'long beards'.

Sarmatians: a non-Germanic, probably Iranian, people who lived along the Danube frontier.

Sax: a large knife carried by most Migration period warriors. It could serve as both a weapon and tool.

Shieldwall: a defensive immobile formation with men standing shoulder to shoulder with overlapping shields.

Spangenhelm: a conical segmented helmet, of Danubian origin, worn throughout this period.

Spatha: a fairly long sword that was the favoured side-arm of the period.

Strategikon: a Roman military manual written at the end of the 6th century.

Tacitus: P. Cornelius Tacitus, a 1st century Roman soldier, politician and historian who wrote about the Germans of his time.

Tervingi: one of the Gothic clans which crossed the Danube in AD 376, later merging with the Greuthungi and some other groups to form the Visigoths.

Vandals: a Germanic people who crossed the Rhine in AD 406, moved through France and Spain, and eventually settled in north Africa.

Vegetius. *Flavius Vegetius Renatus*: a 5th-century writer who produced a military treatise lamenting the demise of the classical heavy legions and urging improvements in training and equipment.

BIBLIOGRAPHY

Ancient sources
Bradley, S.A.J. (trans.), *Anglo-Saxon Poetry*, Everyman's Library, 1982
Beowulf, Penguin Classics, 1957
Cassiodorus, *Variae*, Liverpool University Press
Garmonsway, G.N. (trans.), *The Anglo-Saxon Chronicle*, Everyman's Library, 1954
Ammianus Marcellinus, *The Later Roman Empire*, Penguin Classics, 1985
Mauricius, *The Strategikon*
Tacitus, *The Agricola and the Germania*, Penguin Classics, 1970
Gregory of Tours, *The History of the Franks*, Penguin Classics, 1974
Procopius of Caesarea, *History of the Wars*, Leob, 1979
Vegetius, *The Art of War*

Modern sources
Barker, P., *The Armies & Enemies of Imperial Rome*, Worthing, 1981

Bachrach, B.S., *A History of the Alans in the West*, Minneapolis, 1973

Bachrach, B.S., *Merovingian Military Organization, 481-751*, Minneapolis, 1972

Banting, D.A. & Embleton, G.A., *Saxon England*, London, 1975

Balbi, M., *L'Esercito Longobardo, 568/774*, Milano, 1991

Bona, I., *The Dawn of the Dark Ages*, Budapest, 1976

Boss, R., *Justinian's Wars*, Stockport, 1993

Burns, T., *A History of the Ostrogoths*, Bloomington, Indiana, 1984

Bury, J.B., *History of The Later Roman Empire*, New York, 1958

Christlein, R., *Die Alamannen*, Stuttgart, 1978

Delbrueck, H., *Geschichte der Kriegskunst im Rahmen der Politischen Geschichte*, Berlin, 1921

Dixon, P., *Barbarian Europe*, Oxford, 1976

Dupuy & Dupuy, *The Encyclopaedia of Military History*, New York, 1970

Evans, A.C. *The Sutton Hoo Ship Burial*, London, 1986

Gordon, C.D., *The Age of Attila*, Toronto, 1966

Heather, P., *Goths and Romans, 332-489*, Oxford, 1994

Harrison, M., *Anglo-Saxon Thegn*, London, 1993

James, E., *The Franks*, Oxford, 1988

Jones, A.H.M., *The Later Roman Empire*, Oklahoma University Press, 1964

Junkelmann, M., *Die Reiter Roms*, 3 Vols, Mainz, 1992

Keegan, J., *The Face of Battle*, London, 1976

Lot, F. (trans.), *The End of the Ancient World and the Beginnings of the Middle Ages*, New York, 1961

Maenchen-Helfen, O.J., *The World of the Huns*, Los Angeles, 1973

MacDowall, S., *Late Roman Infantryman*, London, 1994

MacDowall, S., *Late Roman Cavalryman*, London, 1995

Perin, P., & Forni, P., *So Lebten Sie Zur Zeit der Volkerwanderung*, Nurnberg, 1985

du Picq, A. (trans.), *Battle Studies*, Harrisburg, 1947

Pirling, R., *Romer und Franken in Krefeld-Gellep*, Mainz 1986

Taeckholm, U., 'Aetius and the Battle on the Catalaunian Fields', *Opuscula Romana VII*, 1969

Randers-Pehrson, J.D., *Barbarians & Romans*, Kent, 1983

Reichardt, H., *Die Germanen*, Hamburg, 1978

Todd, M., *The Early Germans*, Oxford, 1992

Wallace-Hadrill, J.M., *The Barbarian West*, New York, 1961

Wilcox, P., *Rome's Enemies: Germanics and Dacians*, London, 1982

Wood, I., *The Merovingian Kingdoms, 450-751*, Harlow, 1994

INDEX

Figures in bold refer to illustrations

Related Titles

To order any of these titles, or for more information on Osprey Publishing, contact:

North America: uscustomerservice@ospreypublishing.com

UK & Rest of World: customerservice@ospreypublishing.com

www.ospreypublishing.com

Insights into the daily lives of history's fighting men and women, past and present, detailing their motivation, training, tactics, weaponry and experiences.

Full colour artwork

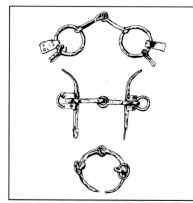

Illustrations

Maps

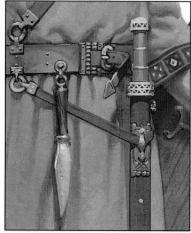

Unrivalled detail

Germanic Warrio
AD 236–568

The 3rd to the 6th centuries saw the collapse of the classical Mediterranean civilization and the emergence of new states in western Europe based on the Germanic warrior society. This book focuses particularly on the men who made up the retinues of the Germanic warlords who carved kingdoms out of the carcass of the West Roman Empire. Although source are scarce, Simon MacDowall constructs a convincing picture using evidence from Roman historians, German archaeology and Anglo-Saxon poetry. The warriors' society, hierarchy training, equipment, appearance tactics and style of fighting are all examined, building a comprehensive portrait of the Germanic warrior during this period.

US $18.95 UK £11.99 CAN $22.0
ISBN 978-1-85532-586-9

9 781855 325869

PUBLISHING

www.ospreypublishing.com